DEDICAT

MW00887697

Missy Serenity Hines for always ⟨
me the freedom to grow and evolve as a person. You are the love
of my life and my best friend. Oh, and thanks for loaning
"Missing Pieces" to me for this book's cover.

SPECIAL THANKS TO MY BETA READERS:

Brittany (Jewish Grammar Nazi) Baker; Maria (Madam
President/Golden Goddess) Bayless; Chris (Night Falls, but Day
Breaks!) Kage; Caitlin (Badass Editor of the Year) Knisley; Kris
(Mean Goat Comics Guru and Editor Extraordinaire) Lachowski;
Heather (Brilliant Editor and Patron Saint) Forrence
Marmorstein; Joe (Joe-Mo Sapien Editor Par Excellence)
Weaver; Ted (I Missed my Calling and Should've Been an
Editor for a Major Publisher) White.

THANKS ALSO TO:

Banshee and Ginger Wildheart Hines: for being such benevolent feline
dictators; Mom: for always accepting and loving your weird son, even
if we have butted heads over religion at times; Dad: for supporting my
writing, even when you don't necessarily care for it; Nick and Mark:
for letting me pester you with questions and for allowing me to use
your real names; Mal Thokey and Stephen Strohmenger; Rafer
Roberts; Eric Adams; Jennifer Hoose; Keri Lovelace; Tracy Salka;
Rusty Hardin; Joseph Morris; Philip J. Lee; Benjamin Nodzak; Cathy
"Spongebob" Leininger; Scott Carlson; Meg Overman; Melissa
Naseman; Bruce Rosenberger.

SPECIAL AUTHOR'S NOTE:

The names of most people have been changed to protect the author's
pasty white ass. While the name of my former band has been changed,
clues have been included that should enable readers to hunt down
evidence of its existence.

Rebirth Defect:

My Journey From Catholic Altar Boy to Teen Atheist to Adult Christian Metal Evangelist and Back to Atheism

By:

Stephen Hines

A.L.B. BOOKS

ISBN-13: 978-1519629708
ISBN-10: 1519629702

Statement of Purpose/Preface Thingy

Okay, let's get one thing straight. _I didn't write this book to de-convert anyone._

Honest.

So, if you're a devout Christian, Muslim, Hindu, Mormon, Catholic, Scientologist, or whatever, you just keep on doin' what you're doin'. No offense, but, as long as you're a good person who doesn't try to shove your beliefs down my throat or protest at military funerals, I really couldn't give a rodent's rectum about your spirituality. It's none of my business. Go to church. Don't eat pork. Worship Ganesh. Pray your rosary. Do...well, whatever the fuck those batshit crazy Scientologists do. Jump on couches and pretend you're on Oprah? Whatever. If it keeps you from going on a multi-state killing spree armed with grenades and an Uzi, knock yourself out!

For your information, I wrote this book, well, for _your_ information. That's it. Over the years I've been asked more and more how I went from being a Catholic to a teen atheist to a rabid Bible thumper (with a mullet!) to a (somewhat) mild-mannered atheist and I've always said, "It's a really long story. I'll write a book about it someday. I promise." Now, after repeating this oath a bazillion or two times, frankly, I'm tired of stalling. So, instead of procrastinating more or becoming rude to (mostly) well-meaning folks who are just curious, here ya go.

I done wrote a book about it.

So if this book offends you, don't launch a campaign to re-convert me. Don't carpet bomb me with hellfire and brimstone e-mails. If you're really pissed off, I'm so nice I'll give you a list of names and home addresses of all the people who've pestered me for the story contained within these pages. So go bother THEM! It's their fault this book exists, not mine!

Incidentally, if you feel so inclined, you can pray for me. That's cool. Whatever lights your altar candles, pardner. That's none of my business either.

Prelude in C (for Crucifix)
Or: Jesus Ain't No Swinger, Baby!

When I was just a three year-old everyone in my family should've known that I was bound to be an iconoclastic prick. You see, at this stage of my toddlerhood I was going through a phase in which I felt compelled to mimic everything my older brother did. If Nick picked up a Lone Ranger coloring book when we were in K-Mart then I had to have one too. If Nick asked for an NFL sweatshirt for Christmas, so did I. Of course, my big bro didn't mind this at first but my parroting quickly began to annoy the shit out of him.

Maybe that's why he set me up the way he did. Okay, he claims that he *doesn't even remember* the entire incident detailed below, but I'm sure you'll see why I suspect him. I mean, we are talking about the guy who stuck a frog gig (a tiny pitchfork used for killing amphibians) halfway through my foot once, after all.

So, one day I waddled into the hallway outside our bedroom to see Nick gently swatting Mom's crucifix, making it swing gently like a pendulum, with our long, thin, yellow whiffle ball bat. I stood and quietly watched while he alleviated his boredom in this sacrilegious manner for about thirty seconds.

5

Eventually he appeared to lose interest so he dropped the plastic bat and walked away. Of course, I had absolutely no clue why he was doing this but that didn't matter. Whatever Nick did I HAD to do as well. Those were the rules, man!

Now, you have to understand that this crucifix was no ordinary, run-of-the-mill, lightweight Catholic statue. This puppy was an official Last Rites (or Sick Call) crucifix. As if having a bloody, suffering savior nailed to two planks of wood decorating our wall wasn't depressing and creepy enough, this crucifix was at least five pounds of religious guilt and fear designed to assist a hurried and unprepared priest if he needed to bless a dying family member. The crucified Jesus lid slid off to reveal a secret compartment containing little, yellowed candles and a glass vial of holy water. This thing was endlessly fascinating to me back then but, as an adult, I can't help wondering how many smugglers around the globe have used such devices to transport illegal goods across borders.

Boarder Guard:

Mornin', padre. Anything illegal you'd like to declare?

Father Cartel Pawn:

No, jefe. Just some holy water and candles. That guy behind me has a few kilos of cocaine in his donkey, though.

Being the little three-year-old Nick worshipper that I was, I just HAD to pick up that whiffle ball bat and mimic his blasphemous behavior. Nothing happened to him so obviously everything would work out great for me, right?

WRONG!

I stepped up to the plate and began gently batting the crucifix into pendulum-swing mode. Apparently it wasn't swinging as much as it had for my brother so I started slapping it harder.

Swat!

Wobble-swoosh-swing.

Wobble-swoosh-swing-swing.

So far so good. It may have flopped around on the nail it was mounted on but that just made for a more entertaining game. Hell, even Nick hadn't demonstrated this much skill and he was the one who invented this sacrilegious sport! If only he were there to witness my glorious one-upmanship!

SWAT!

Wobble-swoosh-swing-swing.

Wobble-swoosh-swing-swing--

KABLAM!

OUCH!

Holy hell! The damn crucifix had flown off the wall and nailed me right in the mouth! I touched my pudgy toddler fingers to my upper lip and felt some warm liquid. The taste of iron filled my mouth. As soon as I saw my unholy blood all over my digits the pain quadrupled and I bawled like the little heathen baby that I was.

WAHHHHHHHHHHHHHHHHHHH!

Of course, Mom came running to see what was the matter and she was NOT pleased to see her blue-eyed baby boy bleeding all over the carpet with a defiled deity in pieces around him. Still, she scooped me up and frantically scrambled to the car. Of course, once she plopped me in the passenger seat and started heading for the doctor's office her motherly sympathy just gushed forth like water from a rock struck by Moses' staff.

HAHAHAHAHAHAHAHA!

Wait!

I forgot.

We're Catholic!

"This would have NEVER happened if you hadn't been mocking God!" she screeched, glowering over at me with murder in her eyes. "You see? He was watching. And this is what you get for disrespecting the Son of God!"

Most of Mom's rant whizzed over my three year-old head but I got the gist of what she was saying: You don't fuck with Jesus, Junior! He'll open up a can of heavenly whoop-ass that you can't EVEN imagine!

The lecturing, of course, continued the entire way to our family doctor's office. How she managed to get me in without an appointment I'll never know. It wasn't the ER, for God's sake. These days I can't get in to see my family doctor without three days' notice. Then again, it was 1972, four years after *Rosemary's Baby* came out, so maybe physicians had a secret drop-in policy for hellbound toddlers.

Nurse:

You say your son did what?! Oh my! Um…come right over. We'll squeeze little Lucifer, er, Stephen right in!

Today Mom doesn't remember if my upper lip was stitched up or if they just slapped a Band-Aid on it. Call it reaping what I sowed, Karma, or simple physics, whatever, but I still have an impressive scar that runs along the right edge of my philtrum. But, it was worth it. As my man Tyler Durden once said, "I don't wanna die without any scars."

Chapter 1

One of my earliest religious experiences took place in a bowling alley. Apparently, according to the movie *Pleasantville*, this was much more common for Americans during the 1950s. To this day I have no clue who'd taught me about the intricacies of intercession because I'm positive I wasn't even in grade school yet, but somebody somewhere had injected the idea into my pasty white head that, if I prayed for something and sincerely believed, God would answer. Of course, a rational adult would know this doesn't mean that the Big Guy in the Sky is a genie who wants His chubby belly rubbed with fervent hands so He can (POOF!) grant you a wish, but I was just a kid.

You see, in Dynasty Lanes, Willard, Ohio's dark, dingy temple of all things blue collar, I'd stumbled upon a clump of fellow rugrats who'd discovered something that incited pure ecstasy. Ever the curious little fella, I peeked in between the writhing bodies and what did I see? The Ark of the Covenant? Stone tablets bearing the moral code for western civilization? Close, but no cigar, Indiana Jones. What I discovered was a swarm of kids vying for a chance to cram their parents' hard-earned quarters into this squat, coffee table-looking thing with glowing primitive, digital tanks dueling to the death within a maze beneath its glass surface. And just like my peers, my eyes saucerized and my mouth gaped in astonishment. Whatever this thing was, it was the most awesome piece of awesomeness ever called awesome so I bolted off to beg my mom for some change to feed this attention span devouring digital god.

Maybe Mom was bowling a particularly shitty game that day or perhaps she didn't see the value in diverting her son so she could focus on improving her score, but I was told to buzz off. No dice. Apparently hurling a heavy, greasy black ball at dingy, white pins in a sport that was probably invented by cavemen was *cool*. But that glowing little box of futuristic heaven in the darkness behind the lanes was *stupid* and *pointless*.

I was crushed. Bummed. Depressed. How could my loving mother not be supportive of my newfound dreams of violent digital glory? Had she gone mad? Were the down and out country tunes echoing throughout the bowling alley brainwashing her against her adorable son? Whatever was causing this serious lapse in judgment, I knew that begging wouldn't change her mind. So I sloughed off to pout and torture myself by watching the other, *more-loved* children bask in the glow of *Tank*.

But I didn't waste much time feeling sorry for myself. Oh no! The lights within that gorgeous hunk of cutting edge electronics before me weren't the only bulbs going off in that beer-sodden shithole. Nobody else could see it but there was a giant, Catholic chandelier of epiphany glowing over my head. I knew I still had a chance if I went over Mom's head. There was someone else who would see my side if she wouldn't.

So I slammed the door of the Men's room open and barreled past the sink and into a stall, locked the door behind me, and took a seat on the throne. It was time to get serious about achieving video game Nirvana! With my brow furrowed in earnest concentration, I closed my eyes, bowed my head, and began praying silently.

God, please. Give me fifty cents to play that game. Lord, I promise I'll be good for the rest of my life. Just, please, make those quarters appear in my pocket.

I paused with bated breath, my heart pounding double time, giving God time to do His thing. Then, like Ralphie in *A Christmas Story* scrambling to open his Little Orphan Annie decoder ring, I wrangled my chubby little fist into my jeans pocket in search of the silver, minted manna. Oh, I just couldn't *wait* to feel those cool, jingling coins! *Tank, here I come!*

But nothing was there.

So I tried again, pleading with even more intensity. *Lord, please, just fifty cents. All You have to do is pop them into my pocket. I only need to play the game once, then I'll be satisfied. Please, God?! Please?!*

Again, nothing. Just my sweaty little paw encrusted with some lonely scraps of lint.

I prayed a third time, desperately trying to block out the noisy people coming and going beyond the Holy of Holies where I sat supplicating. An annoyed man knocked on the stall door and asked just how much longer it'd be for me to take care of business. "Just a minute!" I growled while jamming my hand into my pocket. And, just like the watery bowl beneath my little buttcheeks, my pocket was still empty.

As I trudged out of the stall, the angry, balding man glaring and cursing at me beneath his breath for keeping his bowels waiting was the least of my worries. Tears welled up and my face reddened with disillusioned anger as I rushed past him to the sink. Where was God when I needed Him? Wasn't He supposed to answer people's prayers? Wasn't He supposed to always be there for me, even when nobody else was? I mean, He could turn water into wine but not lint into quarters? What a crock!

Obviously this little incident reveals more about the nature of my naïve, pre-adolescent mind than it does about the mysterious workings of the universe, but ultimately it's an excellent metaphor for my spiritual experiences as a whole. Whoever taught my toddler self this concept of prayerfully asking and receiving had meant well, and the countless others who'd reinforce the message throughout the rest of my life

13

probably did, too. These people were only repeating Jesus' words ("You may ask me for anything in my name, and I will do it." John 14:14).

Yet, even if this statement originated from the messiah's lips, without concrete evidence of results, why believe it? Despite constant reassurance from the Bible, priests, nuns, preachers, and friends, reality never seemed to stockpile any proof to back up Christ's claim. Even after years and years of desperately wanting to believe that there was an omnipotent being in the sky looking out for me, time and time again life revealed that it all boiled down to me either taking care of or not taking care of business. If anything was going to get done, I had to do it. Or, as Mom always said, "God helps those who help themselves." Well, then, what the fuck's the point of God or praying to Him then?

Prayer was and will always be, if you'll excuse the cliché, a perfect example of wishing in one hand and shitting in the other.

Chapter 2

Somewhere in this same time period, possibly a year or two before the Dynasty Lanes incident, I remember attending mass with Mom, my brother, and my paternal grandma (who insists on being called Granny). It was Good Friday and on the way there my elders prepped me for the ever popular, always a laugh-a-minute Stations of the Cross ceremony. They explained that Jesus would be tried, convicted (unjustly), and then crucified for our sins. Honestly, I don't remember if the resurrection was even mentioned, but, and you'll see why here in a minute, it probably wasn't part of the spiel in the short car ride down to St. Joseph's.

So, we arrived at the parish for mass a little early because Granny always insists upon such timing. We walked in, each person dipping his or her filthy, sinner's fingertips in the little bowl (a "stoup") of holy water before making the sign of the cross. Who knows where this wacky ritual came from? I'm sure some scholars claim to know. It probably had something to do with ancient people never bathing and having no access to Purell. Little did they know they were dipping their crusty claws in tepid petri dishes full of Catholic bacteria, then crossing themselves with "holy" death water. And there you have it. That, my friends, is how the Bubonic Plague really spread.

Apparently some modern churches have switched to hands free automatic holy water machines, much like the soap dispensers in public bathrooms, due to concerns over influenza, Swine Flu, and other cooties being passed along throughout congregations. Call me crazy but, if the water was indeed blessed by the power of an all-powerful deity, how the hell could it harbor viruses that could kill the young and elderly? Could it be that these stoups are full of nothing but plain old water that was mumbled over by a guy who thinks he has magical, God-given powers?

Anyway, we followed Granny to her favorite pew and sat down in the dim, stale incense-tinged church. I don't know about the others in our little posse, but I was nervous. That little car seat catechism on the way over scared the shit out of me. Here I was, this hyper-imaginative toddler, in Plymouth, Ohio of all places, getting ready to watch a trial and execution IN PERSON! Why the hell was everybody else so damn calm and smiley about this? What kind of sick fuck thinks killing someone's a party?

Suddenly, and with no disclaimer that the following presentation was just a historical reenactment for the benefit of the faithful, I might add, the priest took the stage (playing the role of Christ) with a deacon (Pontius Pilate's stand-in) and the

16

miscarriage of justice began. For some reason it didn't even dawn on me that this priest looked absolutely nothing like Jesus. The dude was mostly bald, had no beard, and was even wearing priest's robes with a surplice (a scarf-like thing, for you infidels) yet in my peabrain this was indeed the Son of God. Mr. Pilate wasn't even decked out in a toga, but I had no frame of reference for Roman garb at that point.

The so-called trial culminated with Pontius (inexplicably) putting his decision up to a popular vote, like a bad episode of *American Idol*, and the crowd (including Mom and Granny!) cheering for some douchebag named Barabbas to be set free and poor Jesus to be crucified. As a kid with an evil older brother, I knew what it felt like to be blamed for something I didn't do, so the fact that everybody in that joint had piled on the Barabbas bandwagon so quickly was particularly distressing. How would *they* feel in the J-Man's shoes? Christ!

Throughout the rest of the ceremony, my heart pounded as I hoped and prayed these lunatic adults would come to their senses. *Come on!* I thought. *Snap out of your trance, people! You're acting like a herd of mindless sheep!* But no, the bloodthirsty assholes strapped a big old cross on their scapegoat and marched Him past His own sobbing mother. Then the psychos pounded gigantic railroad spikes through his hands and feet before hoisting him up to mock him with a vinegar-soaked sponge. After one last, humiliating poke in the side to make sure

He was dead, they took Him down and to be buried in some cave that was somewhere offstage.

I was horrified. How they do such a thing? How monstrous and barbaric! And everyone was smiling, shaking hands, and swapping stupid small talk on the way out of the church afterwards. *Hey, how's the family? Got another grandbaby in the oven? Wanna meet up for some dinner before going home?* Had they no shame?

Eventually, probably the next time we attended mass with Granny and I saw Father Jesus alive, well, and stuffing communion wafers in people's mouths, it dawned on me that it was all a play. Still, the complete and utter fucked-upped-ness of the story hung over my mind like a storm cloud for ages. Even when I knew the priest was still alive, I just couldn't shake the emotional hangover of sadness and shock from that night.

Other than that, it was a joyful, spiritually awakening call to the priesthood.

Chapter 3

In first grade at St. Francis' Elementary School, the day reading finally clicked for me was a huge milestone. After what felt like weeks and weeks of feeling like a complete imbecile, a brilliantly beautiful light bulb of literacy just popped on and all of the basics suddenly made sense. It was GLORIOUS! After school that day Mom took me to the library and was barely able to get me to leave. *Screw the candy store! Have you seen all these books?! And they're FREE!*

Other than that I only remember one event. But it was a doozie, in a bad way.

On Wednesdays, whether our little cups were full of Holy Spirit goodness or not, our evil teacher, we'll call her Sister Janine, dragged our little ragamuffin asses to masses. That may not sound all that odd or torturous, but close your eyes and pretend you're six or seven years old again. What were you like back then? Better yet, what was the length of your attention span?

Yeah. That's what I thought.

Mass doesn't sound so glorious now, does it?

So, our huge first grade class was sitting in the first two rows of pews in front of the pulpit and Father was delivering yet another *pulse pounding* sermon about something that was way over our heads when one of my little buddies suddenly gasped in astonishment. Every kid around him, of course, immediately whipped his or her head over to see what was shaking. Was it a vision of Jesus or the Blessed Virgin? Was it the Holy Spirit descending upon us like a dove?

Nope.

It was something WAY more fascinating, to first graders at least: a Super Ball! I don't recall what color it was but I do remember it was quite raggedy looking. Some little kid must've smuggled it in as his church chew toy, bit a hunk out of it, then fumbled the precious cargo, never to see it again. *Sucks to be you!* We all thought. *Now we have something fun to do instead of listening to this old geezer's Bible babbling.*

But, there was always the matter of our nutjob nun teacher to contend with. Her temper tantrums were things of legend and none of us wanted to get busted; so we all nodded knowingly, like inmates signaling the passing of a prison shank down the lunch line, to each other while pointing discreetly in Sister Janine's direction as if to say, *This can be done. This fun can be had. Everybody: strap on your poker faces and let's get this party started!*

For the remainder of that service, the rich, delicious taste of Adam and Eve's forbidden fruit became known to us. Let those two nudist gardeners have their vitamin C! We had a fucking Super Ball, bitches! Curt would bounce it over to James. James would dribble it coyly, keeping his noggin pointed at the pulpit, then sling it over to me. It was glorious! Never has a Catholic mass flown by for me with such lightning speed. And we were SO slick and sly that Sister Janine, that sex-deprived slave driver, never had a clue!

Or so we thought.

When we returned to our classroom afterward, it was quickly obvious that the Sis was pissed. As soon as we'd reentered, the door slammed shut behind our tiny butts. Glowering from the doorway with fire in her eyes and brimstone puffing from her ears, Sister Janine barked, "All of you, line up in front of the chalkboard! NOW!"

Our little hearts jumped into our throats and proceeded to produce double bass beats that would make any death metal drummer jealous. *Holy shit! How did she know? We were ingeniously devious. The woman must have eyes in the back of her head!*

Now that I've been a teacher for almost two decades this incident is even more hilarious than it's ever been. Whether it's junior high or high school kids, they're all fundamentally the same. They will do the stupidest crap imaginable right in front of me, thinking they're the James Bonds of stealthiness, and if Stevie Wonder were in the room even HE could tell EXACTLY what they were doing.

Me:

Hey! Stacy! Quit texting or I'm taking your phone!

Stacy:

I'm not texting!

Me:

Oh yeah, do you always have both hands in your purse while mouthing words to people who aren't there?

Anyway, somehow Sister Janine (the Nancy Drew of nuns) had ferreted the truth out of us. She had it narrowed down to the three stooges in row two: Curt, James, and me. The rest of the class sat down. My buddies and I looked at each other, our eyes wider than offering plates. I was told to step forward so, like an idiot, I did. God only knows how she moved so quickly but Sister Janine lunged forward, grabbed my little arm, and swung me as hard as she could into the chalkboard tray. To this day I wince when remembering that cold, hard, metal strip biting into the very top of my six-year-old back.

CRACK!

The pain and shock of this sacred assault must've kept me from seeing what Sister J did to Curt, but I'll never forget what that bitch did to James. Good ole Jim made the mistake of nervously waddling away from the front of the room toward the closet and bending over to tie his shoes. He probably thought that presenting her with such a defenseless target would deter her rage, but he boy was he wrong! Sister Janine, like an NFL kicker from Hell, approached from behind and punted his chubby ass with every ounce of righteous anger she could muster. James lurched and stumbled forward, trying to stop his fall, only to end up crashing face first into the half-open closet on the side of the room. When he pulled himself to his feet and turned around, all of us could see that his face wasn't just beet red from embarrassment and tears. Wooden shelves full of learning materials aren't typically kind to the face, even one as well padded as James' was.

Now, I don't want to give you the impression that all of my teachers in Catholic school were this bad. In fact, all the other five I had were, at worst, boring broomstick-up-the-butt teachers and, at best, kind and compassionate educators who were grossly underpaid and overworked.

Thinking back on this as an adult I can't help but wonder what the source of Sister Janine's rage was. Maybe she was just burned out from years and years of teaching snot-nosed little rugrats for poverty wages. God knows I've seen my share of crispy educators who make far more than their private school peers. That's a lot of hours preparing lesson plans, attending faculty meetings, and grading papers only to receive a slap-in-the-face paycheck, so I can empathize to a certain degree.

Perhaps if the antiquated and misogynistic tenets of Catholicism had allowed her to get married (or at least have a shiny, silver, vibrating boyfriend) Sister J would've had more tolerance. Maybe she longed for the love of a good man and the joy of having a brood of her own. It's also possible that she was a repressed lesbian who fucking hated kids.

Or, maybe she was simply Satan's Fanged Vagina made flesh.

Who the hell knows?

I guess the real issue here is: why were such discipline strategies tolerated? Sister Janine was certainly not the only Catholic teacher who beat the shit out of students. Why else would the ruler-wielding stereotype exist? And, hello! I've read James Joyce's *A Portrait of the Artist as a Young Man*. There's a reason why poor Stephen Dedalus' brutal pummeling with a pandybat struck a chord with me.

Aren't nuns supposed to be the Brides of Christ? Didn't Jesus stress turning the other cheek and treating your neighbor as you'd want to be treated? Didn't he go around feeding, teaching and healing people? Wasn't his message one of love, peace, and understanding?

Ever notice that the people who advertise their faith with the most ostentatious zeal are usually the least Christlike?

Yeah, me too.

Sister Janine taught this lesson to me very well.

At least she taught me *something*.

Chapter 4

If having to go into a musty, wooden box to confess my sins to a priest was supposed to deter me from deviant behavior, the Catholic ritual was an utter bust. Why do I say this? Because, in second grade, we were prepped for our first time of Spilling the Beans on All the Ways You Were Naughty, which paved the way for the Confirmation ceremony that came two years later; see this chapter's postscript. So, nervously and with patient guidance from the priest, I made it through round one. Whew! As I stepped out into the sanctuary I remember wiping my sweaty little palms on my pants and thinking, *Man, this sinning crap just isn't worth all this stress! I'm never doing anything that I'll have to explain in there again!*

[Insert insane laughter here.]

Back then I was painfully shy. Okay, honestly, saying I was painfully shy is the equivalent of saying politicians tend to fib once in a while. I made other shy people look like wildly delirious, nude Bacchanalians swinging from chandeliers while chugging powerful adult beverages. So for me to waddle into that confessional and admit guilt to this high holy sacred ambassador from the big J-Man took massive courage. What the hell I even had to confess at that age eludes me, though.

You see, my introversion kept me quite sheltered and immature in relation to my peers. Still, as I struggled to come up with some mea culpas to whisper through the screened partition, I remember feeling like I obviously was the scum of the earth. What a little dirtbag! I deserved to have my nose shoved into piles of my steaming shit. Otherwise, why would all of the wise adults in my life put so much emphasis on this religious practice? Confession, apparently, was like forcing down that awful medicine that will make you feel better later. The healing power of anything in life is always proportionate to the hideous taste left in your mouth, so the trauma of my first confession certainly purged the unholy fires of Hell from my soul, right?

WRONG!

Not long after that, while in our local shopping mall, I wandered away from the rest of the family to drool over the *Star Wars* action figures. This was right after the toys were widely released to retail outlets and were selling like hotcakes. Certain figures were almost impossible to find due to rabid nerds immediately snatching them up. At home I'd managed to assemble Luke Skywalker, Chewbacca, and R2-D2, but my collection was pathetically malnourished. But my hopes were high that more of these magical toys would be found at the mall that day.

I remember rounding a corner and stumbling upon an endcap display that overflowed with every single character yet released. Each and every black package adorned with the silver, metallic *Star Wars* logo beckoned to come home with me. There was Han Solo with his cocky, smuggler's grin assuring me we'd have plenty of roguish adventures as soon as I reunited him with his Wookie pal. Princess Leia, with her dual-Danish hairdo, begged to help continue the fight against the dark side. But wait! Was that Obi-Wan Kenobi?

The horror of seeing him murdered by that bastard Vader was still painfully fresh in my mind. Wave after wave of sentimental respect and grief washed over me. Sure, he was old when his former disciple cut him down, but he was so wise, patient, and compassionate! There were so many more people Obi-Wan could've helped, if only he'd had more time! As I lifted the packaged Jedi off the display and held it before my beady little eyes, Ben Kenobi pleaded to come home with me. His story didn't have to end on the Death Star, his watery, hound dog eyes seemed to say. Together, we could rewrite his ending. Or we could at least explore his exploits before he got roped into *Leia's* drama.

The problem was that I had no money. And begging Mom almost never worked, unless it was for a cheap piece of crap that came out of a gumball machine, because she knew she'd have to face the music with tightwad Dad when we got home. Nope. She wouldn't cave. For her it wasn't worth it but for me a few hours of parental disharmony followed by the awkward silent treatment was a small price to pay for endless hours of sci-fi bliss.

But what could I do?

A little voice in my head whispered, *Take it! Stuff it inside your coat! It's a big, puffy winter coat. Nobody will know.*

Now, I don't remember receiving much moral instruction about the immorality of shoplifting at home, church or school, but somewhere along the line I'd probably had my hands smacked for trying to take some shiny bauble from a department store or another kid's toy box. There was no prolonged sermonizing on the topic. Still, just standing there with Obi-Wan in my clutches while contemplating theft made my palms sweat and my little heart beat fast and hard.

Some would say these pangs of conscience were the Holy Spirit trying to steer me down the right path, but I'd already sat through a buttload of church and the concept of God and sin or confessing to a priest about taking a five finger discount never once entered my mind during this moral dilemma. No, it was probably nothing more than the fear of a severe ass-whuppin' from my parents that made me shake like a Chihuahua on crack as I snuck looks to either side, gauging if the coast was clear.

And it was.

So I stole it.

Yep. You read that right. I pilfered a prophet of the Force. I jacked a Jedi knight.

Could irony get any more palpable than that?

I think not.

Somehow nobody in that store or at home caught me. I have no idea how my parents didn't notice a new addition to the growing Lucas menagerie in my bedroom. Maybe it's because they were busy working their asses off trying to make ends meet and didn't have time to closely monitor my inventory.

Nah, that couldn't be it.

The point is that the supposedly righteous conviction from a perfect, holy God never seized me. As soon as I got that brown-robed, lightsaber-wielding geezer home the glorious adventures of imagination began.

Guilt?

HA!

Don't make me laugh.

That is until, weeks later, my teacher at St. Francis informed us students that round two of confession was the next day. At first the news of a second session had no effect on me. The rest of the day was just another blissfully ignorant routine. There weren't even any pangs of guilt or dread throughout that evening at home. Nope. No bolts of Holy Lord Lightning zapped my scrawny ass, even during the prayer before supper.

However, as soon as I slithered under the covers and slowly drifted off to sleep: BAM! The mother of all guilt trips pimp-slapped me into terrified consciousness. *You have to go to confession tomorrow! If you don't tell Father what you did, he will know! God tells him everything! And then he'll tell your parents! You're dead, buddy!*

Tossing over to my other side, I clamped my eyes shut and attempted to reassure myself. *Father doesn't know! He can't know! How could he?*

Oh, but he does know! And you know how much trouble it is when you lie and then get busted! Just confess. Beg for mercy. He'll understand.

Multiply that back and forth argument by one thousand and compound it with a full dose of guilt-ridden tossing and turning then you have a pretty good idea how the rest of my night went. It was brutal. By the time I oozed out of bed in the morning, I decided to confess. Throwing myself at the mercy of the Almighty's local customer service rep was the only safe bet, even if the mere thought of admitting to shoplifting made me queasy and jittery.

And I felt all manner of queasy and jittery that morning in school but, fortunately, we were sent over to the church *before* lunch. I mean, you wouldn't want a growing boy to forego his daily sustenance would you? What's more important, a kid's eternal soul or a delicious peanut butter and jelly sandwich?

I rest my case.

Anyway, my shaky, quaky legs carried me into confession as best they could. After sitting I squeaked, "Bless me, Father, for I have sinned."

"And how long has it been since your last confession?" he asked. Did I detect a trace of smug, I-know-you-did-something-naughty attitude in his voice this time, or was I just being paranoid?

We went on reciting our prescribed dialogue until the improv portion of the performance arrived. I didn't want to start out with the Obi-Wan incident, so I started with some more piddly, chickenshit stuff I'd done. Eventually it was no use stalling any more. I had to drop the bomb to get this guilt and anxiety off my chest. Bracing myself for an angry, disappointed reaction like I'd get at home, I sputtered, "I also sh-sh-shoplifted a *Star Wars* action figure."

Through the screen between the confessional booths I heard Father's seat creak. He cleared his throat. *Oh, God! Here it comes! He's going to call Mom and Dad. Then I'm going to be killed. Then Father will have to do my funeral. Then...*

"I see," he calmly replied.

Gulp. Is this just the calm before the storm?

"And where did you take this toy from, my son?"

32

I tried to squirm quietly. *Why is he asking that? Is he going to turn me in?* "Uh...from the Sandusky Mall." *Oh, good job, genius! Now you're definitely going to jail!*

"Does your family go there often?"

Huh?

"Um, I guess so. Every few months." *Yikes! Maybe I should've said every week. Now he's going to really feel obligated to turn me in since we don't go all the time.*

"Well," he sighed. "Obviously stealing is a sin. What I would first advise you to do, young man, is ask for the Lord's forgiveness."

"Okay." My fidgeting nearly ceased. *That's not so bad. I can do that, but what else?*

"Then, it would be wise for you to return this item to the store you took it from and tell them what you've done. Do you think you can do that?"

Take it back and tell them what I did? Are you INSANE?! They'll put me in jail! Do you know what my parents would do to me? Do you want me to die?! "S-sure, Father. I can do that."

When monkeys fly out of my butt!

"Good. Now, say ten Hail Marys and five Our Fathers before you return to class."

"Yes, Father."

Heaving a huge sigh of relief, I stepped out to pray my rosary, as commanded. But the odds of me taking that toy back and confessing to the store management were the same as the odds of St. Francis' Elementary School adopting Darwin's *On the Origin of Species* as a science text.

Looking back as an adult on a foolish, childhood decision, I can see that what I did was obviously wrong, but not because the Bible or a sage-like celibate man dressed all in black says it is. Sure, both of those have had some cultural impact on me, but I've always been the kind of guy who realizes that rules provide structure in life, but, if they don't make sense to me, I ignore them.

Since I've grown up (to what extent is debatable) and worked for a living, it's quite clear that stores pay money for their inventory and expect to sell it for profit, which keeps people employed, etc. So, for me to take their stuff is wrong. And I haven't done it since. Because I know how it'd make me feel if someone did it to me. I guess what I'm trying to say here is: morality ISN'T complicated! The basic rules for being a productive citizen with integrity didn't float down to us from the heavens. Yet one of the most common arguments that well-meaning Christians throw at me deals with this very topic. *How can you know what is right or wrong without faith? The Bible is the basis for all morality in modern civilization!*

Really?

Reread the story of Lot and family hanging out in Gomorrah (Genesis chapter nineteen) then.

If THAT is the basis for how to treat an innocent young lady when there's an angry, mob of rapists lurking about, then I think I'll stick to being a supposedly amoral heathen, thank you very much!

Postscript #1:

According to the Catholic Encyclopedia (yes, it exists and it's FREE on the internets!) the rite of Confirmation is defined as: "A sacrament in which the Holy Ghost is given to those already baptized in order to make them strong and perfect Christians and soldiers of Jesus Christ." That one sentence is so irony-laden and redundant that it doesn't even bare discussion, so I'll move on.

Confession supposedly prepared us for Confirmation, but that wasn't the end of the prep work. We also had to find sponsors (preferably a godparent) to be our mentors and create these oh-so-cheesy red, felt scarves to wear during the ceremony. There were also worksheets assigned by our teacher so our confirmation process could be monitored. On these papers, we had to name some potential sponsors and explain why they were candidates for the job. Then we had to come up with our Confirmation names, which were to be the names of famous saints. The uber-importance of these names was stressed over and over to us. These saints were to be our guides from the great beyond, so we needed to choose wisely! I mean, you wouldn't want to fuck up and take the name of the patron saint of finding parking spots (Saint Thomas, according to some) when you still had a good eight years before you could drive, dumbass! And then there was the worksheet with a diagram of our future red, felt stoles with a bank of holy symbols (doves, flames, crosses, etc.) to choose from. We personalized them by picking the items we wanted, then sketching our symbols on one side of the scarf diagram, leaving the other side for our Confirmation name.

Being a young, naïve little dork, I took this quite seriously. I drew symbols on the diagram, contemplated them, erased and replaced them, then ended up having to get a second diagram because my eraser had worn holes in the stupid paper. Finally, I decided upon a dove (since the Holy Ghost most certainly was gonna descend upon me during that ceremony), a flame (I could already envision a bitchin' fire floating over me for all to see) and, well, none of the other choices looked appealing. But there was so much empty space to fill.

My Confirmation scarf couldn't look all lopsided with a big gaping red hole of dead felt! There had to be one more symbol to add, otherwise my budding artistic sensibilities would have given me OCD shitfits and prevented me from becoming an adequately badass soldier of Jesus Christ! After hours and hours of deliberation, I finally gave up and went with the safe bet: a cross. Besides, something told me all of those stuffy adults wouldn't go for the symbol of the Rebel Alliance from *Star Wars*.

Morons! What did they know?

Speaking of that ragtag group of Vader haters, I was able to sneak one geeky detail into my Confirmation rite. I chose Saint Luke to name myself after. Every time someone would bust my balls over the fact that I obviously chose this name in honor of Mr. Skywalker, I'd dazzle them with my research on the biblical saint's awesomeness as the church's first martyr. *The dude was stoned to death for not denying the big J.C.! That's why I chose him! I'm not THAT much of a nerd. It has nothing to do with Star Wars. Shut up!*

Of course, no one even pretended to believe that nonsense.

After all the hype, pomp and circumstance leading up to my Confirmation ceremony, I distinctly recall feeling pretty gypped that no white dove or flame was ever visible in the sanctuary. There was no warm, spiritual buzz imparted to me and, for all the pressure about choosing our Confirmation name wisely (because it'll be your second middle name that will stick with you forever!), within two weeks tops every single one of us kids forgot all about the new label and never thought about it again.

I haven't been able to stand big, overblown formal ceremonies ever since.

Postscript #2:

Also, according to the online Catholic Encyclopedia, the oil smeared on our foreheads (by a bishop) during the Confirmation ceremony is called "chrism".

I bet you wish you could unlearn that factoid.

Chapter 5

Fortunately, after Sister Janine, my other teachers were bastions of tranquility. Most were, as previously mentioned, either quite compassionate or duller than two dollar latex paint. My guess is any student of any age would take either of those types over a psycho nun any day! Well, except for a creepy S & M guy with a nun fetish, of course.

In second grade I had a pretty and sweet younger teacher, we'll call her Mrs. Perez, who had the patience of a saint. Most of that year is a blur for me, but I do remember that she had a calm, quiet voice and it took a lot to frustrate her; but, even when upset, she did a great job of holding it together.

For example, I remember finding out that a classmate, Sandy, had a crush on me. While the concept of romantic love was about as much a part of my thoughts as musings on the philosophical underpinnings of modernist literature back then, I do remember feeling some butterflies while making doe eyes back and forth with Sandy. That is until one day when we were divided up into pairs and spread out all over the classroom to do some math exercises. We had these tiny, squat, round electronic gizmos (picture a mini bowling ball crossed with the Apollo

Lunar Module) that were supposed to make math fun and exciting. Maybe it was kicks and giggles for my classmates, but I've always enjoyed the subject with numbers as much as explosive diarrhea, so primitive computers did nothing to ease my pain.

After groaning in agony, I flopped belly first on the classroom's thin, institutional, vomit orange carpeting and, in between glancing over at Sandy, blushing, and giggling, began working away with my partner. Eventually we all settled down, forgot about socializing, and immersed ourselves in the learning exercise. Of course, as soon as we were finally on-task, some quiet giggling started in the far corners of the room. Eager to get this numerical nastiness over with, I kept my eyes on the prize and kept chugging along. *Get thee behind me, Satan! I gots numbers to crunch!* But then the giggling began to get louder and louder and less and less secretive. Pretty soon, full-fledged guffaws erupted, breaking my trance and forcing me to look around for the source of the class' amusement.

I swiveled to my right. All the kids on that side of the room were red-faced and looking behind me; some were even pointing brazenly. Twisting my torso back to the left, I quickly discovered the source of my peers' hilarity. There, looking like she wanted to tunnel through our classroom floor straight to Lucifer's lair, was my crush, Sandy, with a giant urine stain on the front of her pants.

Oh no! That's so gross! I thought, torn between being repulsed and empathetic.

Mrs. Perez rushed over, whispered to Sandy, then whisked her away to the restroom while glaring menacingly at the laughing hyenas being left behind. I can still see the look on Mrs. P's face. It was obvious that she was boiling with rage. She may have been a sweet, soft-spoken woman with a heart of gold, but kids also knew not to push her too far. There was an invisible line of respect drawn in the sand, and we had just crossed it. Well, technically I hadn't joined in on the chucklefest, but my gaping eyes and mouth didn't exactly mark me as a non-participant.

For the entire time Mrs. Perez was out of the room there was stunned, fearful silence. Usually a teacherless classroom is a festering Petri dish of anarchy, but not that day. Sleeping crickets would've sounded as loud as a fifty-car pileup in there.

Finally, Mrs. P returned but Sandy wasn't with her. The poor kid was waiting in the office for her parents to either come get her or deliver fresh pants. I'm pretty sure they just took her home for the day, but it was entirely too late to salvage Sandy's reputation. In that tiny parochial school in little ole Willard, Ohio hick town, an event like that created a label as indelible as Hester Prynne's scarlet A. To her face kids would call her Sandy. Behind her back she was forever referred to as Pisspants. Try living THAT nickname down!

41

We were scolded (rightfully) and punished, but the exact nature of the lecture and consequence is lost in my Swiss cheese memory. The fact that we were all receiving a moral, religious education had little to no impact on either our reaction to poor Sandy's dilemma or our admonishment. It was as if none of our brains retained or used data from the daily biblical instruction we received. There was no inclination to treat this poor, urine-soaked classmate as we'd want to be treated. No one even made an effort to comfort Sandy, except Mrs. P. Sadly, nothing but our petty human nature was on display. A room full of immature homo sapiens fell back on the evolved tendency to follow the herd. We laughed, pointed and mocked because one little brat at the top of the second grade social hierarchy started it.

Does that make it right?

Absolutely not!

But that same herd mentality saved our rear ends when Mrs. Perez gave us a vicious tongue-lashing. She, as the respected leader of our little pack, let us know that this social behavior was inappropriate and wouldn't be tolerated. As soon as the first tiny mackerel snapper in the room lowered his or her head in shame, the rest of us followed. We didn't even think about humiliating a classmate when she was around.

Notice that last phrase: when she was around. Out on the playground or on the bus, Sandy was still fair game because Mrs. P wasn't there to instill fear or respect. That's pretty messed up, isn't it? Anyone who says morality isn't subjective is full of shit and about as self-aware as a turnip. Kids can be evil little bitches and bastards, especially if they know they can get away with it.

And it's the same with adults. Life, for most people, involves testing the boundaries to see what's allowed and what's punished. How else would you know that it's possible to drive seventy-two miles per hour in a sixty-five zone without getting pulled over? Isn't the speed limit sixty-five? Yes, but we've learned that cops and state patrol troopers will usually bend that far and no more.

But are the ideas behind Catholic schoolteachers and law enforcement officers what forces us respect these boundaries? Did that classroom full of second graders bow their heads in shame during Mrs. Perez's angry lecture because we knew God was disappointed in us? Do I drive no more than seven miles per hour over the speed limit on the highway because I worship the United States government and all of its assorted appendages?

HELL NO!

We hung our dorky little melon heads because we respected this lady who taught us every day. She had earned our respect through daily displays of firm yet fair leadership. Every kid in that room had a heart heavy with grief over letting Mrs. Perez down. She never approached her lessons half-assed or treated us like crap, so what gave us the right to disappoint her this way? Our guilt had absolutely nothing to do with divine conviction. When push comes to shove human brains don't consult *Yahweh's Etiquette Manual From On High*, AKA The Golden Rule: "Do to others as you would have them do to you." (Luke 6:19). We non-sociopaths become conditioned through nature and nurture to either behave responsibly (i.e. what's best for the pack/society) or act like piss-midgets because an authority figure is spineless and doesn't follow through.

As for my driving habits, I'm no anarchist but I guarantee that the reason I don't blaze down the interstate at supersonic speeds has nothing to do with a patriotic love of donut-munching Taser wielders, or a sense of loving devotion for my fellow humans for that matter.

HELL NO!

If it weren't for $180 speeding tickets my ass would be qualifying for NASCAR!

YEEHAW!

And, as further proof that kids are little shitheads, after that incontinence incident, Sandy and I were done. Finito! El done-o! There was no way I was dating someone with the nickname Pisspants!

Chapter 6

My third grade teacher at St. Francis Elementary, Mrs. Ringer, was a woman with the personality of boiled, sauceless spaghetti. She wasn't a bad teacher; she was just boring. The only thing I specifically remember about this somnambulant wonder was her reluctance to let us use the restroom.

But Mrs. Ware, my fourth grade teacher, was amazing. After Mrs. Ringer's dusty delivery almost anyone with a pulse would've been nice, but our tiny class' expectations were certainly exceeded that year. Mrs. Ware wasn't spastically entertaining but she radiated compassion, understanding, and a love for teaching.

You've probably heard this wise saying: "People won't remember what you did. People won't remember what you said. But people will always remember the way you made them feel." Those three sentences are the perfect distillation of Mrs. Ware's class. I can't remember specific lessons or, for the most part, conversations from that class, but I'll never forget that students felt valued and respected in that room.

Most teachers in religious schools don't exactly welcome questions about fossilized church dogma. If you want to infuriate a Christian educator (or man/woman of the cloth) just try asking questions like: "How did Adam and Eve's children reproduce without committing incest?" Or: "If we all came from Adam and Eve, how'd we get folks with black, yellow, red, brown and white skin?" Just be sure to step back before the frothing saliva starts flying your way as this person of faith showers you with the wrath of God.

But Mrs. Ware wasn't like that at all. She created such a welcoming atmosphere that, during the class' religious instruction, we felt secure enough to risk almost any query. Did she always have the answers? No, but she never pretended to be all knowing. She would calmly take advantage of a teachable moment and attempt to lead us to a logical answer. There was never a single ounce of condescension or insecure annoyance in her voice.

Make no mistake about it, if someone becomes irate in the face of questions about his faith, it is certainly the result of insecurity and fear. If a person is defensive even toward different sects of her religion, let alone completely foreign belief systems, ignorance and self-doubt are the causes. When just the thought of someone being an atheist causes the faithful to truly lose their shit, what does that reveal? A hidden anxiety that maybe, just maybe, there's no one up there to hear their prayers? And to someone who's never had the courage to truly, deeply examine the facts or their feelings on religion, what could be more terrifying?

Recently I've gotten back in touch with Mrs. Ware, thanks to Facebook. I made it a point to thank her for being such an understanding, open-minded teacher. Out of respect for her beliefs I avoided mentioning that I've been an atheist for twenty-four of my forty-four years on this earth. I tend to avoid bringing up the subject anyway (what's ruder than bringing up politics or religion in polite company?) but, if the person I'm conversing with has a deep, calm and secure faith I never want to do anything to offend them.

Honestly, those people are very rarely the ones to bring up the subject. Their faith is embedded in their very molecules so there's no frenetic need to proselytize or sprinkle phrases like "Praise Jesus!" or "Bless God!" all over the conversation like a fidgety dog pissing all over to mark his territory. Does Mrs. Ware ever express her faith on Facebook? Sure. Does her every post or communication deal with the topic? Absolutely not. She's secure in her belief. It's no more necessary to constantly broadcast this than it is to reassure the world that she's a woman.

Truthfully, though, I avoid bringing up the subject around insecure believers as well. I know how I feel when someone pushes his beliefs on me: disrespected; and, since I hate that feeling more than almost anything, why make another being feel it?

But, if a believer gets in my face over my lack of belief, all bets are off. If you make your faith my business in a rude way, prepare to be treated in kind. This rarely happens (except on the internet where everyone seems to have balls of steel) so it's easy to continue leading the born-to-be-mild lifestyle that I prefer.

Chapter 7

The rest of my elementary school experiences were mostly unremarkable. In fifth grade we drove one teacher to a nervous breakdown (this experience plus my own substitute teaching at this level have convinced me that kids at this stage of development need an old priest and young priest!) and the lady who replaced her barely made it out alive as well. So much for religious instruction taming the human beast.

My sixth grade teacher, Ms. Ferraht, was a crotchety old former nun who left the sisterhood for a priest she'd fallen in love with. This Romeo of the rectory eventually ditched her to return to his calling. Maybe this is why she seemed to hate boys. All of us were stuck paying for that damn priest's fickleness. Doesn't seem fair, does it? Neither does the fact that we're all (supposedly) stuck dealing with original sin, but apparently we're all guilty by association.

When my older brother, Nick, had Ms. F it was a match made in Satan's smoky lair. I don't know what he did to torture that poor woman but he eventually pushed her to the point of slapping his face. When Mom found out she charged in like a five foot nothing ball of fire. It was recess when she arrived and all of us were lining up to march back inside. Ms. Ferraht, I'm sure, regretted not getting her class rounded up faster. Mom glared in her face (okay, more like into her chin area due to a slight height discrepancy) right in front everybody and, in uncharacteristically clean language, warned Ms. F that, if she EVER hit Nick again, there would be hell to pay. To this day I can still picture that old hag's gaping, terrified face. It's one thing to be an unforgiving witch when dealing with children and another to keep clutching that broomstick while facing down an angry parent.

Two years later the jilted ex-lover of a priest had to deal with me. Ms. F must've seen my name on the class roster and immediately began preparing because she shredded me like a bad check on the very first dreary, rainy morning of sixth grade. And what was my unforgivable sin? Did I walk in and call her a hippo-hipped, wart-nosed, spell-casting crone? Did I whip out my dick and piss on her floor while screaming, "This is for smacking my brother, Nick, BITCH!"

Nope.

Back then I was a quiet, timid little people pleaser. So, instead of some filthy, cardinal sin, my offense simply this: I walked into Ms. Ferraht's room, my windbreaker soaked from the dismal drizzle outside, and immediately hung it in the coat closet, then sat in a seat.

"Mr. HINES!" she bellowed, making me jump roughly six feet out of my seat. "What do you think you are doing?"

Shaking like a fiending junkie, I replied, "Uh...I just hung up my coat."

"And?" she growled.

Was this a trick question?

"And I had a seat?"

"Exactly! Who told you that you could be seated? That is NOT your assigned seat! And who gave you permission to hang your coat up?"

"Uh...nobody did, Ms. Ferraht." *I just thought it was wiser than dripping puddles all over your classroom floor.*

Her thick, demonic eyebrow arched and her misshapen face twisted into an evil grin. "Correct. Now, please retrieve your coat and stand at the back of the classroom until further notice."

Of course I did as I was told. For the most part I had yet to begin questioning authority. Still, the whole time I was reclaiming my coat and walking away from that closet the only thought in my mind was: *What a hag! It's the first day of school. All I did was hang my stupid windbreaker on a hook and sit down. This is gonna be a LONG year!*

Fortunately, even after this awkwardly tense start, my pasty white charm eventually (somewhere around the end of the first semester) melted Ms. F's icy exterior and we grew to like each other. Middle-aged women have always taken a shine to me. What can I say? At one point I even remember being embarrassed about accidentally becoming the teacher's pet. I don't think any of the other kids busted my chops for it but, being the shy guy that I was, the attention was *not* welcome. Plus, people with low self-esteem (and I had virtually none until my twenties) don't handle compliments very well and tend to downplay them. It did make me feel good to be told that I was smart and creative, though. Most adults just told me to get my head out of my ass and grow some common sense.

To this day I wonder if the irony of the situation (the person who was supposed to teach me to "judge not lest ye be judged" automatically assumed I was Nick 2.0) was ever apparent to Ms. Ferraht. Even if it never was she still taught me a valuable lesson in what NOT to do as a teacher. Whenever I'm tempted to dread (or rejoice about) having a former student's sibling, old Ms. F's gnarled visage comes to mind. It's even better than a slap in the face as far as reality checks go. Apples may not fall far from the tree but they *can* roll in opposite directions from the parental trunk that spawned them.

Hell, just look at my brother and me!

Chapter 8

There are two final Catholic school anecdotes that I absolutely have to share. To not do so would be both incredibly selfish and inhumane, and I am nothing if not a selfless humanitarian.

At the beginning of the year at St. Francis Xavier Elementary School, all sixth grade boys were drafted into altar boy service. We were simply informed that Father Marcus had drawn up a schedule for all Wednesday morning masses and any unforeseen ceremonies (i.e. funerals) would be decided on a case-by-case basis. Of course, we all were *orgasmic* at the thought of putting on red or black dresses topped with billowy white blouses in order to be subjected to the violent temper tantrums of our current, perennially pissy priest.

Who wouldn't?

You see, Father Marcus was a rather round, balding fellow who was a little too enthusiastic about drinking his savior's blood on the job. During mass, after saying the prayer to bless the little stale cardboard wafers and altar wine, magically transforming them into a gourmet, divine cannibal feast of Lamb of God steak-crackers and vital juices, the priest served the congregation. After all in attendance had partaken of the holy sacrament, Father was supposed to scarf down the leftovers and clean out the communion plate and chalice. Now, most ministers would slurp down the one or two surplus drops of wine and then rinse the cup out with water and towel dry it before moving on. Not Father Marcus! That sanguine fella always filled the chalice all the way back up, pounded down the sacred sauce, refilled it, and had an encore. As we all know, some folks are happy drunks and others are downright booze bastards. Father M. was almost always a bisected nose hair away from a tantrum so it's pretty safe to say he fell into the latter category.

One such priestly paroxysm occurred when several of us youngins were being trained for our first funeral mass. It was a bright, sunny morning and I was unexpectedly yanked out of class, along with a couple friends, to meet Father Marcus in the sanctuary. The ruddy reverend must've been a little hungover because he barked just about every instruction at us as if we were in boot camp and it was his job to whip our sorry behinds into shape. First we, my buddy Mike and I, had to line up on either side of him at the back of the church. Then we were supposed to march down the aisle in perfect step while holding candles on sticks as Father trailed behind us.

Now, I've never been the coordinated one in my family. While my brother inherited all of the athletic ability and excelled at any sport he attempted, I could (and can still) hurt myself while walking or sleeping. Plus, I am the oh-so fortunate recipient of such glorious genetic blessings as high blood pressure, prostate and sinus infections, horrible eyesight, an anxiety disorder, depression, high cholesterol, and scoliosis.

Other than that I totally got a *fantastic* deal!

Anyway, the whole marching-in-perfect-time-while-carrying-a-burning-candle-on-a-stick-that-could-potentially-dribble-scalding-wax-on-me-thing wasn't exactly something I took to like a pedophile to priesthood. Our first attempt was a train wreck. By the time we waddled like drunken ducks past the third or fourth row of pews, Father Marcus was screaming and spraying an intoxicating saliva mist while lurching toward us. All Mike and I could do was stand there, frozen in place and gaping in fear while clutching our giant candlesticks in death grips.

Of course, I wasn't standing there for long because Father injected his lardass between us and shoved both of us as hard as he could in either direction. Thankfully I wasn't hurtling through stale incense-tinged space for very long because my ribcage served as a super duper breaking mechanism as it collided with the decorative end of a wooden pew.

CRUNCH!

Lightning bolts of pain shot through my right side and I yelped like a kicked dog. So what happened to the other altar boy? When I looked up, tenderly cradling my ribs and fighting back tears, I saw poor Mike picking himself up between the opposite pew's seat and kneeler. When he gingerly turned around his face was beet red and his thick spectacles were tragically askew.

Of course, Father Marcus showed all kinds of penitent remorse for assaulting two sixth grade boys, right?

FUCK NO!

He just kept bawling us out and gesticulating like a madman because we weren't lining back up for another practice run. Eventually Mike and I got it right. How we were able to concentrate on marching while wounded and fearful is beyond me, but we carried on like good little prepubescent soldiers for Jesus Christ.

Kids are resilient that way.

*

Sometime later in the year I was scheduled to serve a regular Wednesday morning mass. There were two other classmates on the roster as well: my cousin Mark and a kid named Derek. Being the geniuses that we were (obviously we learned nothing from the incident I just described above), the three of us hatched a plan to *enhance* our altar boy experience. Backstage at the church, the sacristy to those in the know, there was an unlocked cabinet with a glass door full of crunchy Eucharist and room temperature altar wine. Since those cardboard-tasting wafers didn't do much for us, we were on a mission to have a go at that vino. We knew Father Marcus always took his sweet old time arriving to slither into costume before the big show, so we hauled ass over there as early as possible. Once we arrived we stood, tittering like nervous schoolgirls, trying to work up the courage to commence Operation Serve Mass While Buzzed.

"But what if we get caught?" I whined.

Derek scowled. "Quit being such a pussy!"

"Yeah, Stephen," added Mark. "Grow a pair."

"A pair of what?" Yeah, I wasn't exactly cutting edge back then.

Finally, after a good five minutes of bickering and snickering, Derek, being the ringleader in this endeavor, ever so quietly popped the cabinet open and slipped a bottle out. He turned around, holding the wine out for us to examine. I remember being secretly disappointed because the bottle's label was just an ordinary liquor sticker. It was just wine made by some corporation and sold to churches. Finding that out really cheapened the sacrament for me because I'd naively expected it to have a top-secret direct-from-the-pope or 100% Blood O' Christ tag on it or something. This crap wasn't any different from the Strawberry Fields pink stuff that Mom occasionally had in the fridge.

How lame!

The costume and prop room of the sacristy was connected to a larger, main backstage area by a narrow hallway and, for some reason I can't recall, Derek suggested that we adjourn there to partake. Maybe he was hoping that the change of location would alert us that an adult was entering the building sooner. Who knows?

Once we arrived we formed a triangle (the unholy trinity?) dead center in the room. For a second or two we took turns looking at the bottle and into each other's deliciously fearful eyes. Ooooh! This was scary, ballsy stuff. We weren't just sneaking some booze; this was *God's* booze! This was forbidden AND fermented fruit. We were going to be elementary school legends!

Derek twisted the cap off slowly while Mark and I gasped. Again, we all gawked nervously at one another. It was so quiet we could almost hear Jehovah dusting off His scales of justice to weigh our little slimy souls for the afterlife.

Finally, Derek lifted the bottle to his lips, closed his girly-eyelashed eyelids, and gulped some wine down. As his Adam's apple bobbed one last time, he slowly, blissfully opened his eyes and held the bottle out to Mark, who smiled, took it, and chugged some himself. Then it was my turn. I tipped the bubbly back and gulped some down. Surprisingly, the distilled essence of God was very sweet, fruity and not exactly top shelf quality. A pleasant, warm sensation slowly spread through my belly as I completed the circuit by passing the wine back to Derek.

Once again, Derek clamped his eyes shut and raised the bottle. This time he was *really* going for it, sucking away like a hungry puppy on his mommy's teat. The problem was, Mark and I were gulping ourselves, for air that is. We squeaked impotently, breathlessly, and desperately trying to get Derek's attention. He was oblivious lost in the alcoholic embrace of the Fisher of Men. And behind him stood the angry, hulking mass of Father Marcus.

And by the feathery, dovey-dove wings of the Holy Ghost was that priest PISSED!

Before we could warn Derek, his scrawny, wine funnel neck was being throttled from behind by Father Marcus. I kid you not, the padre came damn close to lifting that kid off the floor. But Derek's eyes didn't stay closed long! That poor bastard's peepers popped open and bulged like a Pomeranian with his nuts caught in a bear trap. I could almost picture the headline in the *Willard Times*: Altar Boy Murdered for Bogarting Alcoholic Priest's Wine.

Eventually Father's ham-hands released Derek in order to snap that blessed bottle away and shove him toward us. It took a few seconds for Marcus regain his power of speech, but that gave our crimson friend Derek a chance to regain his ability to inhale oxygen.

During that agonizingly awkward period of silence we braced ourselves for the impending nuclear onslaught. Here comes the pronouncement of eternal damnation, precluded by phone calls home, leading to unimaginable, slow torture at home as well as school. Ms. Ferraht's demonic antennae were probably pulsing and throbbing with Father's psychic commands for corporal punishments previously unheard of. She was definitely pushing the giant red button hidden beneath her grade book then scrambling down the steps into her secret lair full of medieval torture devices left over from the Inquisition.

We.

Were.

SO.

DEAD!

"Do you three know what a privilege it is to serve mass? DO YOU? DO YOU?" Father Marcus bellowed as his head spun 360 degrees and pea soup vomited all over the room.

We gulped, too afraid to even nod.

"I can't believe you have the audacity to drink this wine! What the HELL is wrong with you?"

The gulping continued.

"What do you have to say for yourselves? Huh?" Now his eyes were bugging. *And it couldn't be healthy for an obese alcoholic's face to turn THAT shade of purple, could it?*

More gulping.

For once in our little smart alec lives we had absolutely nothing to say for ourselves, thankfully.

"Now, all three of you are banned from serving mass in the parish for the next five weeks! You hear me? FIVE weeks! Being an acolyte in the house of the Lord is an honor. I want you to think about what it is that you've done during this suspension. FIVE weeks! And then, if you're lucky, I'll let you come back. You hear me?"

Yeah, Father. We get it. Five weeks. You've said it about eighty times. Just go ahead and drop the real *hammer on us. Let's get this over with.*

"Now, get out of here. Go back to class! And I'd better not hear about you causing any more trouble or your parents WILL be called!"

It took a few moments for that data to be processed.

Our noodly legs carried us out the Sacristy's door and onto the sidewalk to the school. Once we were outside in the bright, warm sunshine we stopped, reformed an unholy triangle, and blinked in disbelief.

Wait a minute! Are you kidding me? "THAT is our punishment?" I exclaimed.

Mark numbly shook his head. "Yep," he squeaked.

Derek's cocky smile slowly crept back onto his lips. "Holy shit, you guys! We just got busted drinking altar wine and the

61

only thing that happened was we don't have to serve mass for FIVE weeks!"

"HELL YEAH!"

Not only was Father Marcus a complete asshole to work for but he was also, obviously, completely clueless on punishing wayward kids. But there was NO way we were going back in there to beg for a real consequence. We were stupid but not THAT stupid! How the hell could a grown man think that banning us from the worst form of Catholic schoolboy torture (well, other than being diddled by a priest) was in ANY way, shape or form a punishment that fit our crime?

Does a complete lack of sexual contact with women lead to a massive sperm clog that impedes blood flow and in turn causes the priestly brainpan to overheat, killing precious brain cells? Or had his advanced alcoholism achieved this result on its own? Perhaps it was a tag team effort. Maybe Father Marcus was just like a lot of people who can't remember (even faintly) what it was like to be a kid and then become teachers.

I see you smiling and nodding. You've had some of those douchenozzle teachers, haven't you?

It's possible that there are men who become priests because they imagine it only involves a cushy, peaceful routine of advanced Bible study, prayer, and occasionally interrupting that ecstatic schedule to sleepwalk through the monotonous, stagnant play called "mass" for a half-empty church full of dusty old farts. Just like there are folks who become educators because they just LOVED school because it was so EASY and they were always the kids who raised their hands and spouted CORRECT answers in between NEVER getting in ANY sort of trouble WHATSOEVER.

Gag.

Barf!

Both priests and teachers in this situation probably find themselves trapped by the security of the vocation they've chosen while growing increasingly bitter about the fact that these cushy jobs aren't *remotely* easy. In fact, they're both frequently thankless, exhausting, and downright taxing. And many of those people in the pews/desks couldn't care less about the homilies/lessons they've worked so hard to prepare for them! In fact, those ungrateful vermin keep repeating the same damn sins/errors over and over again, showing no signs of progress at all. Nobody said anything about this in seminary/college!

ARGHHHHHHHH!

Probably the main lesson I've taken away from Father Marcus is that, regardless of what religion is being professed, or title a person has been given, or uniform he is wearing, no one is worthy of my respect or emulation unless they've EARNED it. I couldn't give two shits if you're the Pope and you wear conical hats and live in a massive palace in Rome. You still burp and fart just like me, pal. You are not God's chosen mouthpiece on this here planet. You're just a regular Joe with the same chances (mostly) on this earth to do right or wrong. Both of us can choose to either use our authority to help and nurture or let it go to our heads and lord it over the so-called peons beneath us.

And none of us should ever, EVER continue on our career paths if we're living lives of pure hypocrisy.

Am I perfect?

HELL NO!

I never claimed to be. And I sure as HELL would never beat or psychologically abuse a kid for making a juvenile mistake.

But I can also guarantee that I'm too smart to punish a kid by banning him from the task he dreads most. I would've made the wine-swilling sixth grade me serve every last sweaty, un-air conditioned mass for the rest of that interminable year.

That would've kept me from sneaking another man's booze!

Chapter 9

Well before I'd ever heard of a badass existentialist named Henry David Thoreau I was already fond of long, philosophical hikes in the woods. When I was five, my family moved to a little development outside the Willard city limits called Holiday Lakes. All of the little bodies of water out there were man-made but, back then at least, that didn't stop them from being great places to swim, fish, and ski. Plus the land around the lakes wasn't overly developed yet so there were all kinds of shady woods to explore. Of course, there was virtually nothing else to do out there, but, in retrospect, I'm grateful for that. The solitude was almost always therapeutic and it forced me to grow an imagination.

Toward the end of sixth grade and into the summer, my budding pubescent mind began to strike out in search of its own identity. I began going out for longer and longer hikes by myself, just losing myself in nature and letting my thoughts wander at will. In the woods there were no nagging adults to boss me around, nor was there an older brother to call me a sissy or beat up on me. I was free to do whatever I damn well pleased with nobody to scrutinize or criticize me for it.

And it was AWESOME.

Add into this mix the fact that my favorite literature to read was mythology and a wonderful, bubbling potion began to simmer in my brainpan. Whenever we drove the five long miles into town I checked out a couple more volumes of the adventures of Zeus, Poseidon, Perseus and Icarus. It's my belief that heroic, mythological adventures are even more appealing to someone growing up in the sticks where there's nothing to do but chores to ease the boredom. While hiking in the woods I'd pretend to be on a quest for some magical talisman of the gods that would save my village from a destructive monster. Any fallen branch became a sword from Mount Olympus to be used to fend off skeletal soldiers or lop off Medusa's snake-infested head. Eventually I even pretended to be Indiana Jones fleeing through the jungle with a glorious archeological find while being pursued by indignant tribesmen who were being spurred on by a Nazi mastermind.

And the magical, cerebral potion continued to bubble and froth.

Somewhere along the way, my immersion in global folklore, while only motivated by a young boy's thirst for adventure, lead to my little peabrain detecting patterns in the books I was devouring. Every culture had stories about how the earth and its inhabitants were created. They all had humans who fell from grace and then were punished by the god or gods, both

66

on earth and the afterlife. And many of these yarns, I discovered, had quite a bit in common with the doctrine I'd been taught at home, church, and school.

So, while traipsing through the forest or resting on a rock beside the lake, I'd ponder what all these similarities meant. If there was only one true God and one true church (the Roman Catholic Church, of course! Duh!) then why did all these assorted tribes from all over the globe seem to be explaining the world around them with parallel tales? Was it because God chose to reveal Himself in a multitude of ways to all these different countries out of sheer annoyance at repeating the same damn story over and over? *Ya know, if I have to tell the big boat full of animals in a flood story ONE more time I'm just gonna stomp all these pissants back into mud!* Or was it simply a case of primitive homo sapiens with underdeveloped brains and no scientific knowledge whatsoever trying to comprehend the universe and their part in it? *Why it bright in day but dark at night? Gods put moon fire in sky for nightlight. They scared of wolves, too!*

The more I thought about it the more the former sounded ridiculous and the latter made sense. Incidentally, this epiphany created no animosity toward organized religions of any stripe but it did, ever so quietly and gently, sway me over into atheism. I had no urge to argue or de-convert anyone. I had no idea if anyone else in the world had arrived at the same conclusion. It was just a case of shrugging and deciding upon a different philosophical path. At the time it wasn't any bigger of a deal than choosing to eat a bologna sandwich instead of peanut butter and jelly.

Still, there was absolutely zero chance that I'd tell Mom or refuse to go to church. I'd had an epiphany, *not* a sudden death wish! Again, it wasn't even important enough to even necessitate any kind of symbolic gesture to declare my non-theism, unlike my oh-so dramatic conversion to born again Christianity at the age of nineteen, which we'll get to in the following chapter.

Today, writing and thinking about this evolution in my thinking process makes me wonder if I should consider my earliest, pre-Catholic school years an atheist time period as well. I seriously doubt that any infant pops out of his mother's birth canal thinking that the bright light ahead is Jehovah, Allah, or Zeus. There isn't any way our brains could have any information about any culture's pantheon at that point. Science is just now discovering that we do have an inherited, primitive animal sense of right and wrong encoded in our DNA, though. We can comprehend concepts of sharing, fairness, family, safety and danger almost instantly. But it isn't until we're absorbed into the fabric of our family and community that we even become cognizant of religious concepts.

Until then, life is just life. I cry when I'm hungry and those huge, blurry people who take care of me supply food. I sleep when I'm tired, which is most of the time because that vaginal exodus was freaking exhausting! Eventually I have to cry again when nobody gets the hint that I've shat myself and don't want to wallow in my own excrement. Giggling and smiling makes me and those around me happy, so I to do that a lot. Screaming and bawling annoy them into some form of action, too. It's so easy to get my way when I have all of these weapons in my arsenal!

Life was never complicated until all those supposedly grown-up concepts of sin, guilt, damnation, atonement, forgiveness, and salvation came into play.

Ah, hell. I'm just going to chalk up my first five years on earth as my first gloriously godless era. Then I enjoyed another seven from ages twelve to nineteen.

How, you ask?

That, my friend, is a story for another chapter.

Chapter eleven, to be exact.

Chapter 10

In the previous chapter I mentioned that my descent into the unholy abyss of atheism wasn't grounds for any rebellion against my family's Catholicism, and initially it wasn't. But by the end of my eighth grade year, thanks to my brother being on the high school football team, I became a fan of the glam metal band called Motley Crue. Nick brought their *Shout at the Devil* cassette home and at first I ribbed him by saying things such as, "What the heck is this satanic crap you're listening to?"

He wisely didn't take the bait. Instead he simply shrugged and said, "It's what we listen to in the weight room."

To provide some context, I need to clarify that my listening tastes at the time were no more intense than Huey Lewis and the News or Prince and the Revolution. Of course, the more I listened to *Shout* the more it grew on me. But before you jump to the conclusion that I'm blaming rock n' roll for my teenage rebellion, I'm not. It's natural that teens gravitate toward rebellious art when going through this stage of development. We all have to separate ourselves from our parents' values, find out who we are, and then decide if we want to endorse the norms that have been presented to us. I had already started to quietly question and dismiss these values so the next logical step was to become outwardly defiant, and thus the Crue's shock rock demon seed found fertile soil.

At first I merely started wearing Motley's black t-shirts and reading every interview with or article on them that I could find. We didn't have that there internets back then so I was totally at the mercy of the shitty magazine selection in Shitkicker, Ohio. Needless to say, info was scarce and incredibly out of date even when it was available. Then, during my freshman or sophomore year in high school, I had a giant *Shout at the Devil* back patch sewed onto my denim jacket with a fiery pentagram that I insisted on wearing to mass. Even my older and WAY wilder brother questioned my sanity on this issue.

"Stephen, you sure you wanna wear that to mass? What's Mom gonna say?" Nick wisely inquired.

Snarling my best Nikki Sixx F.T.W. (Fuck the World) snarl, I growled, "Yeah, I'm wearing it. So? What're they gonna do, kick me out? Big deal! I hate going to church anyway. It's stupid!"

Nick, ever the go-along-to-get-along type, just shook his head and went on with the day. But if Mom was ever ticked about the satanic back patch being on display in the house of Yahweh, she (nor any of our fellow parishioners) never said anything. She was probably wise enough to know that forbidding me this little, juvenile demonstration of anarchy would make it escalate into worse behavior. Ignoring it would keep the powder

71

keg's fuse smoldering without being fully lit. If only the people who constantly show up to picket the latest shock rocker's concerts had this wisdom. As soon as you tell a teenager something is forbidden that kid will sprint toward it so fast his tennis shoes will burst into flames, thus making said shock rocker wealthier, and all-powerful in pop culture.

For the longest time the Crue back patch in church was my biggest rebellion toward religion, but eventually I graduated from high school, thus making me WAY smarter than any adult on the planet. Clearly the 'rents were done telling ME what do to do!

Case in point: One Sunday morning Mom shook my shoulder to wake me for mass. Nick was way over in Texas with the Air Force bossing him around, and Dad never went to church except for weddings and funerals, so it was just me and The Madre.

"Stephen, you going with me to church this morning?"

Knowing full well, even in my sleep-addled state, that this was a rhetorical question, I rolled my mulleted head away (oh, so brave!) and said, "No. I'm just gonna stay home." What cracks me up about this even after all these years is that eighteen year old me honestly thought she'd just be a little miffed but would let it drop.

Damn lazy kid! I'll let it slide this week but NEXT Sunday he's going!

But she knew that by the following Sabbath, a precedent would have been set and it'd get easier and easier to wear her down on the issue. Soon I'd be sleeping in every weekend and be blissfully unchurched!

WRONG!

Remember, I was facing away so I couldn't see Mom's face but, judging by the tone of her voice, I'm guessing she magically morphed into the archangel Michael, head warrior of God's Angelic Soldiers (or G.A.S. for short), with giant, fierce, razor-tipped wings and a halo that was white hot with anger.

"WHAT?"

A bolt of G.A.S. lightning shot through my innards.

Oh shit! She wasn't going to let it fly. Gulp!

"Um...I said I'm tired and I wanna sleep in." I tentatively rolled over and *really* played up my sleepiness. "Just this once? I have to work three to eleven tonight."

Her wings and halo were in stealth mode, but now there were fire and brimstone cataclysms in her pupils. "As long as you live under MY roof you are going to church *once* a week, young man! Now, get your ass out of bed and get ready for church. When you move out and have a place of your own you can do whatever you want, but I don't want to hear ANY more about not going to mass. If being Catholic was good enough for my grandparents and parents, it should be good enough for you! GOT IT?"

Oh, I got it alright. It was time to shut the fuck up and pay lip service to being on board with the papal program. Nothing more was said for quite a while about backsliding from the One True Faith, for a while at least.

Chapter 11

So how did a teenage atheist get lured back into the warm but suffocating embrace of Christianity? Behold, a perfect storm:

Just before graduation I announced my genius plan to take six months to just work and save up for college. Okay, I really kind of *had* to take that time off because my head was lodged so far up my ass that applying for college didn't occur to me until it was too late to register and start on time. But don't tell my parents that. They both still think I started late in a rare demonstration of fiscal common sense.

Shhhh! Mum's the word!

You know how most people revel in that short period between being done with classes and the day they finally receive their diplomas? For me, this down time was more of a curse than a blessing. Even without school, this purgatory period of my life wasn't very kind. My brother, whom I'd hated for most of my life, became one of my best friends in the year before his departure for boot camp. When he left I missed him so much it was crushing. We wrote letters as much as possible but this did little to alleviate the pain.

Plus, I'd started dating a coworker at my grocery store job; we'll call her Joy (because of her correlation to a trailer trash ex-wife on the classic TV show called *My Name is Earl*, not because of the emotion her memory elicits). It didn't take long before I was madly in love with this girl and she, very convincingly, claimed to reciprocate. There were many cuddle sessions overflowing with professions of undying love and marathons of spit swapping. She was the one! I just KNEW it!

But then she didn't bother to show up for my graduation party. The knife in my heart over that was magnified massively by the fact that I'd been asked a million times when my girlfriend was coming so my family and friends could meet her. To say I was embarrassed is like saying getting a colonoscopy without pain medication is a slight pain in the ass.

And the maraschino cherry atop that shit sundae was Joy telling me that she was dating another guy the entire time she was professing her undying love for my mulleted ass. Of course I broke all communication off immediately, but after weeks of silence, her begging me to talk to her again, I, like the imbecile I clearly was, finally gave in. What did she want? To apologize for being an evil, two-timing skank?

NOPE!

Being the spoiled rotten princess daughter of a redneck family from Attica, Ohio that she was, she wanted me to fight this other guy for her. Apparently that was her big fetish in life. Some people turn to crazy entertainment like, oh, I don't know, BOOKS when they live in Hicktown, Ohio. Others resort to cruel psychological head games pitting man against man in a duel for womanly affection. That Spam-eatin' tramp should've had a reality show called *Joy's Trailer Trysts*! Too bad they didn't exist back then.

But, I'm not bitter. Not at all. Mainly because Joy's harlotude freed me up to meet the love of my life.

Add all of that heartbreak together with post-high school fear and anxiety about WHAT THE HELL AM I GOING TO DO WITH MY LIFE and you have one sloppy, sloppy mess. All I had in my life was my shitty grocery store job that had recently become even shittier thanks to vicious rumors Joy was spreading about me, which caused so-called friends to openly turn on me. So I started drowning my sorrows by pounding down my dad's Coors Lite like it was fine champagne. Dad kind of half-heartedly complained that his beer was disappearing while he was at work but as long as I wasn't driving drunk he didn't really care or seem to notice that I was self-medicating.

Truth be told, Dad would've cracked down on my drinking but feeling torn up about Nick being away at boot camp distracted him. One day he stumbled upon me as I was sitting on my bed and weeping pitifully about the chewed up chunks of my heart that Joy had spit into my face. He thought I was crying over missing my brother, so he sat down on the bed and sobbed with me. I didn't have the heart to tell him the truth. It was one of the few bonding moments we'd ever had and I was an aching, lonely, lost mess. Any comfort was appreciated.

*

Fast forward to the winter of 1988: I'm sofa surfing and watching a rock concert on TV, wishing desperately that I had a band of my own. I'd only been playing bass guitar for a couple years, but music was my entire life and having some other guys to jam with would've gone a long way toward filling that giant hole in my life. If only...

RING!

The phone on the stand at the end of the sofa startled me out of my reverie.

RING!

"Hello?"

"Hey, Stephen, what's up, man? It's Gino." Gino was the lead singer of the last band I was in, so hearing his voice was a balm to my ears.

"Dude! How's it goin'?"

"Not bad, man. Not bad. I've been talking with Mark about starting a new band." Mark is my cousin, but not the one I'd served mass with in Catholic school. "And we found this keyboard player named James who wants to jam, too."

"Oh yeah?" *Keyboard* player? Was Gino going soft on me? No self-respecting metal band had keyboards! Still, I was so desperate for a band I'd have sprinted out the door to jam with a fucking polka ensemble at that point.

"Yeah, he's really good. And he can sing, too. Only problem is he's kinda religious."

I'd been listening to Stryper (1980s Christian glam metal band, in case you don't know) for a while and had even seen them in concert once. In fact, I was sent to the principal's office for wearing their *To Hell With the Devil* concert shirt. Apparently wearing satanic Crue apparel (and a Kiss jersey with tits hanging out all over it) was acceptable, but a Bible thumping, bumble bee band's shirt with the word "Hell" on it?

Not so much.

"He play any Stryper?"

Gino chuckled. "Yeah, he's big into them. He likes Journey, too."

"Journey? What the hell?"

"Yeah, his taste in music sucks, but he's really good. Hopefully we can get him to play some real rock. You wanna jam this weekend?"

In music, sometimes desperate times call for desperate *measures.*

"Hell yeah! What time?"

Gino, Mark and I showed up on a brisk December afternoon to jam with James. After lugging our gear into his house, we then had to haul it all up some rickety, winding wooden stairs into a cramped room that was partially crammed with dusty, disused junk. Mark set his drum kit up against a wall with ancient, yellowed farmhouse-style floral wallpaper while Gino plugged his little practice PA and microphone in beside a drafty old window with a killer view of the house next door's top floor. I sat my amp up against the wall opposite of Mark's kit and proceeded to tune my bass.

During this whole process we were all attempting to make awkward conversation with James, treading on eggshells and trying to avoid cussing or bringing up any topics that might offend a short, curly-headed, mustached Christian keyboardist with a Journey fetish. To the best of my memory the topic of religion was mostly avoided during that jam session. We just played bits and pieces of classic rock songs that we knew or could fake until each tune dissolved into discordant chaos. During our last number I distinctly recall getting increasingly angry due to my own mistakes. I'd try to improvise some bass licks while the others held down the chord progression but I was rusty and, on top of it all, my picking arm kept cramping up. Worst of all, at this time I still had virtually no self-esteem so any little error, especially one that would embarrass me in front of people, brought out the bitter perfectionist in me, which only lead to more mistakes and frustration.

Finally I couldn't take it anymore and barked, "Shit!" while punching my bass. My face was as red and hot as a sunburned baboon's ass cheeks. As soon as the word flew out of my mouth I was mortified. I had just met this James guy but he'd been pretty cool so far. Hell, he even apologized when he excused himself for a smoke break, explaining that he knew smoking was wrong and that he needed to quit. Thankfully, I seemed to be the only one who noticed my little temper tantrum and the afternoon ended with everyone committing to another jam session on the following weekend, hopefully with a guitarist on board to fill in the gaping holes in the songs.

*

Gradually, this casual jamming with James became more and more serious, and not just musically. At first Gino and I were just humoring the guy about his religion in order to have someone to rock with but soon, after Gino bailed on the situation (possibly due to the thumping of Bibles, but I can't remember for sure), I began soaking up James' message like a pasty white sponge. Unlike Gino, I hadn't been raised in a hyper-religious family that forbade practically everything; so it's easy to see why he ran for the hills and I didn't. He'd heard enough of that fire and brimstone bullshit as a kid; I hadn't.

Soon an old friend named Bill played with us for a while but couldn't hang with the preaching during jam breaks either. On one hand it was too bad because Bill was one hell of a guitarist, but obviously I can see his point now. Most rockers just want to crank out some tunes without being guilt-tripped for their assorted vices; plus, he came from a really rough life on the streets and had even less patience for establishment bullshit than most musicians.

Sure, I had a bit of a rebellious history but I was in such a vulnerable spot that any situation providing positive ego strokes was attractive; and, despite the hellfire and damnation sermons that were beginning to flow my way, I did feel accepted and valued. James gradually lured me into the fold by assuring me that I wasn't being judged, just encouraged to think about my eternal destiny. Over and over I was reminded that one never knew when the Grim Reaper was coming and, if my soul wasn't right with the Lord, my ass would be cooking in Hell's barbecue pits forever.

Then James *really* got me thinking with a story from his teen years. Apparently he had a really sweet car that had become his golden calf. This glorious automobile was washed, waxed, and buffed more than a twelve year-old's freshly throbbing boner. It became such an idolatrous obsession that God, who's mighty jealous, decided to eliminate it. So, on one hot summer night an angel was dispatched to Attica, OH to recalibrate his priorities. Did this heavenly messenger speak to him in a dream, dispensing a loving warning that would save his teenage soul?

Nope!

Yon angel instead totaled the vehicle without harming the young driver. Well, that's how James told the story at least, and it really hit home with me because I knew that music was my golden calf. What if I couldn't reign in my idolatrous obsession and God made me lose my hearing? The very thought brought visions of suicide to mind.

As for James' life lesson from above, I've heard of people totaling vehicles and walking away unscathed, but the whole "God was so green with envy that He sent an angelic pimp-slap my way" thing is quite laughable. How can an omnipotent, omniscient deity wracked with a petty, human emotion like jealousy *not* sound ridiculous to a rational brain? If every horribly tragic event such as a devoted Christian dying at a young age can be explained with "God's ways are not our ways because He's so far above our tiny, finite perspective" then how the fuck can Jehovah be excused for jealousy?

Talk about a lame-assed double standard!

He's like a controlling, abusive boyfriend who beats his lady for spending time with her friends instead of waiting on Him hand and foot. Only, instead of yelling, "Stop shoppin' with that whore girlfriend of yours, git yer bitch ass in the kitchen, and make my supper!" God annihilates whatever or whoever is competing for His attention.

Of course, I didn't even question this theological atrocity at the time. My fragile emotional state at the time was still ensuring that my ability to think objectively was suspended like Han Solo in carbonite.

*

Sometime during this period James also regaled me with a cinematic masterpiece of 1970s filmmaking that watered the seed of fear that his car crash story had planted. This *big* budget Christian propaganda cringefest was called *A Thief in the Night*. The movie starts with a girl waking up to find that the rest of her family, along with millions of other God fearin' folk, have been raptured away to Heaven. She, being the godless little strumpet of the clan, is trapped on earth during the reign of the antichrist and must try to survive the horrific mayhem after the Heavenward Holy Hoovering.

If you ever get a chance, do look this flick up on YouTube. The whole family can enjoy the entire pulse-pounding giggle-a-minute film for FREE! There are end times believers being fed to guillotines, neon red fake blood, sermons every other frame, and (GASP!) tons of killer 1970s fashion crimes. And that's not all, folks! If you act now this movie will inject the melodic strains of "I Wish We'd All Been Ready" into your brain FOREVER! Even a full lobotomy won't get that shit stain song out of your grey matter!

PRAISE THE LORD!!!!!

And soon I was doing just that.

*

When I got home that night I couldn't shake the fear of living through the antichrist's reign of terror. So I shut my bedroom door, turned out the lights, knelt down beside my bed and prayed the prayer of salvation that James had taught me.

"God, I am a sinner," I whispered in the darkness. "I accept your son, Jesus, as my lord and savior. Please forgive me and come into my life. I need you."

And I felt absolutely no change at all.

Zero.

No choir of angels singing.

No glowing warmth in my heart or gut.

No filthy sins being cleansed from my soul by the blood of the Lamb.

Nada.

Maybe I did this wrong? I thought. All of my Catholic upbringing taught me that there were very specific, memorized prayers to use for almost all occasions. So I tried again, attempting to say the prayer exactly the way James had. This time, I added some extra guilt sauce to the recipe, attempting to really concentrate on and FEEL all the sins I'd committed. Maybe if I really focused on what a scumbag I was and wrung out some salty sinner tears there'd be different results.

Still no change.

I felt exactly the same.

I was still the pathetic, Dumbo-earred, Pinnochio-nosed, mulleted failure of a nerd that I was just a few minutes ago. I was still stuck in the limbo that exists between high school and college, heartbroken and alone without my big brother or a woman to love.

So I gave up, shrugged and crawled into bed. I'd done the best I could. If God was that freakin' picky about everything then there was no way I was good enough for His program anyway. What about all that stuff James had said concerning coming to Jesus just the way I was and being accepted? Wasn't Messiah Boy supposed to give me a big hug and help me start over no matter how rank the stench of my sins?

Eventually, after tossing, turning, and over-analyzing it for hours, I decided that my overly dramatic imagination had built up false hopes for the conversion experience. Just because Saul was blinded by the light on the road to Damascus in true Hollywood fashion, that didn't mean all righteous revelations were the same, right? Now that I thought about it, hadn't James cautioned me about expecting a lot of bells and whistles?

Oh yeah, he had.

Either way, whether I'd just been rescued from the pits of Hell or not, I decided to keep this to myself in case it didn't take. Nobody needed to know about this little religious experiment. The odds were definitely against me succeeding at anything in life, based on my nineteen years of experience, so why set myself up for *more* public ridicule? In the meantime I'd just keep watching for any internal or external changes that might indicate that redemption had indeed occurred. If a pattern emerged that indicated God was somehow on my side now, then I'd go public. If my shitstorm of an existence continued to be miserable I'd just move on and cut my losses.

How scientific!

Unfortunately for me and any other person in this situation, those who are desperate for signs from above quickly become quite adept at finding (more like CREATING) them. Our brains are hardwired to find patterns in our day-to-day lives because this usually assists in our survival and, couple that with a hyper-emotional state, some religious brainwashing and a desperate need for any sort of acceptance, and suddenly life seems to be overflowing with miraculous messages from God.

Even though I thought I was objectively testing this salvation theory, I really was just acutely attuned to any and all mentions of God. If I was carrying a little old lady's groceries to her car and she threw a "God bless you!" my way, it was a sign. If I was flipping through the boob tube channels and a big-haired, flailing preacher (always accompanied by a wife wearing six-inch-deep makeup and even bigger hair) then God was attempting to convey a message to me. If I read the Catholic Bible I was given at confirmation and a verse made me feel a little warm and fuzzy inside, the Holy Spirit was whispering in my ear. When my toast popped out of the toaster with a peculiar burn design, it was Jesus spreading the gospel through singed bakery goods!

HALLELUJAH!

Praise the Lord and pass the margarine!

Looking back, it was really no different from a plaintive horoscope fanatic finding accurate predictions in his daily forecast. Those things are worded in such a generic way that, if you're prone to believing, confirmations of your belief will always be plentiful: "Someone will say mean words to you today, but pay no mind to that big meanie-head! The sun will part the clouds and happiness will return to your life like a rainbow farted out of a unicorn's gloriously ghostly bottom!" "Well, I'll be damned! My horoscope was right! Evil Boss Man yelled at me this morning, but later, at lunch, I DID see the sun in the sky!"

Never mind the fact that horoscopes are studies of celestial bodies' alignments and how they supposedly affect our day-to-day existence. These theories were invented around 3000 BCE (when the stars were in a different place in the sky) by humans with virtually no scientific knowledge whatsoever. How many other beliefs do we cling to from that era? Why would you seek guidance for your day-to-day life from such primitive philosophy? If you're going to seek wisdom from hunks of rock or hot balls of gas then why not pose questions to your pet rock or light your farts? The answers are in the flames, my friends!

Oh, because that would be STUPID!

Silly me!

Finding God's fingerprints all over daily events could also be compared to hypnosis. Studies have been conducted that prove that only certain people (70-75%) can be hypnotized because they are susceptible to suggestion. For this group of folks, hypnosis can help quit smoking, overcome phobias, and regain lost memories. I've even read about a man whose body was covered with hideous warts who was gradually able to invoke the power of his mind over matter to get rid of them, which makes me wonder if this is what really happens during so-called faith healings.

As for me, I tried hypnosis in an effort to combat my social anxiety disorder and avoid taking medication. As luck would have it, I do not fall into the category of being susceptible to hypnotic suggestion. For a while I convinced myself that the hypnotherapy was working, but it quickly became evident that I was fooling myself. Desperate times can make even the most logical among us lie to ourselves and do kooky things. And I am certainly not the most Spock-like dude around, I'll tell ya that.

But, back in 1988, my conversion did serve the purpose of stabilizing my chaotic existence, at least for a while, which enabled me to sprout some badly needed confidence. Plus, as I've already mentioned, excessive drinking had become a coping mechanism and becoming a protestant Christian teetotaler probably kept me from falling into the trap of alcoholism.

Unfortunately, this unhealthy habit was replaced by other, less deadly ones which inhibited personal growth and caused countless other problems.

Chapter 12

One evening, during a break in jamming, I came out of the Christian closet to James. He was pleasantly surprised and his voluminous praise ensured that I was enveloped in a warm cocoon of love and acceptance. No, sickos, we didn't hug and make out. Don't you know that God hates homos?

SHEESH!

But all kinds of advice was offered to me, the newborn in Christ. There were warnings about backsliding (falling away from the faith) and admonitions to find a church where I could feel comfortable while studying God's inerrant Word. I soaked the wisdom up like a human Bounty quicker picker upper paper towel and vowed to do everything I could to embrace and live by these words. I was, after all, a new man. Old ways, including my family's generational devotion to Catholicism, would be cast aside.

*

The first Protestant assembly I attended was the Church of the Nazarene. I picked this place because I had gone to their youth group with my best friend (whose family were hardcore members) a few years back. Back then I was feeling the need for a personal revival--to get deeply and spiritually in touch with my maker, so to speak.

Okay, it was really a desperate (and entirely unsuccessful) attempt to pick up socially awkward, desperate girls whose overprotective parents hadn't taught them that all boys are only trying to get in their pants. But I wasn't lying about my efforts to get deeply, personally in touch.

Still, even though my motives in the past were dubious at best, I had always felt very comfortable there. Everyone was really laid back, nice, and polite. It wasn't the most exciting church to attend (better music, meatier sermons, and fewer ancient rituals than Catholicism) but James had emphasized the comfort factor and warned against picking a place because of its bells and whistles. The Nazarenes were too old-fashioned and resistant to change to even entertain the concept of bells or whistles (AKA snake handling, flopping around the floor, etc.) thus their house of worship seemed like a great place to start.

So I showed up one Sunday morning and, after the service, cornered the pastor to ask how to become a member. I was so naïve that I thought applying for membership was the very first step. Oh, silly me! Out of the mouths of babes! After nervously making my inquiry, Pastor Mike's politely strained expression made it (mostly) obvious that my approach was like asking a girl to marry me on the first date. How the hell did I know? I was *born* into my previous church! Christ on a cracker!

A few days later I met with him in his office and explained that I'd been born again. He asked some thoughtful questions about why I didn't want to attend the church I was raised in, why I chose their church, etc. It was like a surreal job interview and, in retrospect, it almost seemed like he didn't want me to come aboard the *Good Ship Nazerpop*. Maybe he knew my mother and was terrified that she'd kick his ass for stealing her baby boy from the Pope. Maybe my flowing, stylish mullet was a little too radical compared to the snoozing silver-hairs to whom he usually preached. Whatever his motives were, he still put me through an initiation process that required me to become a regularly attending, probationary member.

*

Mom must've felt a disturbance in the Force because I was immediately interrogated before I'd even gone back for a second visit to the Naz. Prior to my first Sunday service I had told her that I was going to be visiting a different church. She was pissed but let it slide, quietly noting that I'd been spending a lot of time at James' house. She also expressed concern over my new friend being eight years older than me so I had to assure her that there was only praying and jamming, no boozing or drugging, going on. In Mom's defense, my last band was inhabited by mostly older dudes who'd kept the practice room stocked with adult beverages that were shared with the two minors in the band. And I may or may not have driven home completely hammered drunk once. But I can neither confirm nor deny these accusations.

Of course, all of my reassurances about my newfound teetotaler state didn't matter one iota once a church change was initiated, so I was cornered very soon after my second dalliance with Protestantism. "Where did *you* go to church today?" Her crossed arms, clenched jaw and ominous tone made it obvious that this was being taken VERY personally, even though I'd assured her that it was nothing serious. I wanted to do some ecclesiastical exploring.

"The Nazarene church where the Tillers go." *Man, she's pissed!* I thought. *Calm. Must remain calm!*

"And why did you want to go there?"

Gulp.

"I told you I just wanted to check out different churches to see what else is out there."

Her eyebrow arched. "So, the church you were brought up in isn't *good* enough for you now?"

"I didn't say that, Mom. I just--"

From there I was given a righteous tongue lashing of epic proportions, during which I bit my tongue both literally and figuratively, until the confrontation finally ended with me losing my temper and informing her that I didn't want to be Catholic anymore.

"Why?" she demanded, choking back tears.

"Because I get absolutely nothing out of the services," I replied, conveniently omitting the part about using mass time to mentally practice my typing exercises during my sophomore Typing class (which lead to me being the second fastest, I might add) and occasionally scoping out the babes who'd also been forced to attend. Then we shouted back and forth for a while longer until I stormed off to my room and Mom stomped off in the other direction.

The following weeks were filled with the patented Catholic Mother Silent Treatment and Evil Death Ray Glares™ that could've melted plastic rosaries at a thousand paces. But, I stayed strong because, dammit, I was eighteen now and she couldn't force me to do jack shit anymore!

*

After a couple weeks I thought Mom had cooled off and was going to let her last bird in the nest fly off to explore while hoping I'd return to the Papal Nest of my own cognition. She'd finally resumed speaking to me, even if her sentences were clipped and sounded like a furiously constipated person's attempts at taking a dump, and the flames in her pupils had faded to simmering embers. So all I had to do was stick to my guns and ride this thing out.

WRONG!

On one afternoon, as I was relaxing and enjoying a peaceful day off, the phone rang. Mom answered it then promptly yelled for me. *It's for me? Who the heck's calling me?* I shrugged and took the receiver. "Hello?"

"Hello. Is this Stephen?" an elderly female voice inquired.

"Um, yeah. Who's this?"

"This is Sister Martha from St. Francis. How are you?"

Sister Martha? What the fu—oops! Can't say that anymore! "Uh...I'm fine," I squawked.

"That's good. Listen, Stephen, your mother asked me to give you a call. Is that alright? Do you mind if we speak for a bit?"

My face reddened with embarrassment and anger. I'd been set up! I looked Mom's way, but she was studiously avoiding my gaze by suddenly developing an intense interest in picking up around the house while staying conveniently within earshot. *Great! She's sicked a freakin' nun on me! I knew she was mad but holy crap! Well, I'm kinda stuck so let's get this over with.* "I guess." *Here comes the guilt trip speech of a lifetime.*

"Good. Now, your mother has expressed concern over your recent decision to leave the Catholic Church so I agreed to chat with you to get your side of the story. Can you tell me why you're leaving?"

My guts churned and my knees knocked. I may have just been born again, but that conversion had only been three or four weeks. As born agains go, I was still a knobby-kneed, wobbly Bambi on an icy pond. The Roman Catholic Church had over eighteen years' worth of baggage stored in the closet I'd crawled out of. You don't just ditch your fear of pissed off priests and scary, mean-assed nuns overnight!

Numbly, I said, "Well, I've just been feeling like I don't get anything out of mass...for a long time now. And, it's not that I don't want anything to do with God. I just want to find somewhere that I belong." In my mind I could see Sister Martha sounding a silent alarm, alerting the Vatican's Apostate Squad of ninja cardinals (armed with crucifix nunchucks and Virgin Mary throwing stars) while nodding her head and tapping a ruler with a sharp, steel edge against her palm menacingly. I braced myself. *Here comes the pain, White Boy. Hold on tight!*

But, surprisingly, Sister Martha didn't let loose with a maniacal tirade about evil, ungrateful teenage bastards who ditch the beloved church that was good enough for generations and generations of their parents' families. Instead, she calmly asked a few more spiritual questions, gauging my sincerity, then proceeded to tell me that she saw nothing wrong with what I was doing. In fact, she felt it was quite normal and natural. Then she asked to speak to Mom again.

Still shaking but now slowly descending into a posttraumatic state of shock, I handed the phone over and shuffled off to my bedroom to recover. Once inside my sanctum sanctorum, I gently closed the door and pressed my ear against it. All I could make out were muffled snippets of hushed conversation. This HAD to be a setup. There's no way that nun was letting me off the hook that easy! Those two were surely cooking up an ingenious mind control plan to reel me back into the Mackerel Snapper boat. Hell, if peaceful techniques didn't work ole Martha would probably club me with a crucifix and send me off to some secret monastery specializing in reprogramming deserters via holy waterboarding.

After what felt like decades, I finally heard Mom hanging up the phone. By the time she'd walked from the living room to my bedroom I was already sprawled out on my bed, innocently pretending to be immersed in reading the Bible. She couldn't *possibly* murder me while I'm studying God's Word, right? Nobody is that heartless! As the door creaked open I felt my heart pounding in my chest as a cold sweat broke out all over my body.

At her infamous throat clearing signal, I looked up, careful not to stare too long into her fiery gaze. "Well, I talked with Sister Martha."

I gulped. "And?"

"She said that, as long as you're going to church somewhere, that's what's important. And if it's meant to be that you come back to the *One True Church*," she added. "You're always welcome." Something told me that the part about the One True Church was a touch of artistic license on Mom's part, but I wasn't about to open that can of worms.

Instead I stammered out a bunch of reassuring nonsense about how Sister Martha was totally right and that it didn't matter what building I parked my posterior in on Sundays as long as I was seeking God. Mother let me babble for a while before chiming in with her final words.

"I don't necessarily agree with Sister Martha, but I guess there's nothing I can do. You're not a kid anymore. I just want you to know how much this hurts me." Tears welled up in her eyes as she shakily finished with, "Just remember that you're breaking your mother's *heart*. And maybe God will bring you back someday."

As the door closed and her loud sobs and soft footfalls sounded in the hallway, my head crashed down onto my Bible. It was the very definition of a bittersweet victory. While I was indeed off the hook, technically, the price was to be paid in the currency of guilt. Lots and LOTS of guilt. And NOBODY (Well, other than Jewish matriarchs, of course) can dish out guilt trips like Catholic mothers.

*

These days, what's fascinating to me about this is the fear and anger most Christians feel when a friend or family member expresses an interest in another denomination. I can see why they would flip over a child suddenly converting to a violent, radical Islamic terrorist cell's ideology, but why the panic and rage over switching to a slightly different flavor of the same religion?

Part of the reason has to be based in one of the biggest points of pride indulged in by almost all organized religions: WE have the correct answers to the puzzle of life. If you don't endorse every iota of our dogma, then you're just going to burn in Hell forever and ever. OUR truth is better than *your* truth. Nanna nanna boo boo and nyah nyah nuh nyah nyah!

How is this any different from Missy and I arguing about the proper method of folding fabric? As freshly married youngins, we endured the agony of the laundromat, or as I like to call it: Purex Purgatory. On one fine Saturday afternoon, my lovely bride chastised me for my sloppy towel folding technique. "Stephen!" she yelled, snatching the offending object from me. "That's *not* how you fold a towel. Do it like *this*."

Rolling my eyes, crossing my arms, and not remotely paying attention to her method, I replied, "Dear, what's the difference? Either way, one of us will yank the thing out of the closet, scrape it across our wet bodies, and hang it up to dry. Which towel will get better results, yours or mine?"

Sighing the sigh that not so secretly means, "My husband is a royal dumbass", she again insisted (and STILL insists) that her way was the *only* way and proceeded to reteach her lesson. Meanwhile, I daydreamed about NFL football, crushing heavy metal guitar riffs, and, *possibly* getting even by holding her down and farting on her head.

Yeah, it was probably that last item.

My point is this: anyone who thinks life is *always* one-size-fits-all should be avoided. If Missy had the "no way is correct except mine" attitude about anything more important than towels, you can bet your sweet patootie we'd never have lasted as a couple. And, when people first get married, they tend to make the mistake of arguing over stupid shit like this, but those who make it work (usually) outgrow this juvenile attitude and instead develop the art of compromise. Isn't family supposed to be about learning to get along?

Then why do church families always seem to fail at it when they've supposedly been transformed by the love of God? Before you claim that they don't, why are there so many different denominations of Christianity? Because someone had the "my truth is right and all others are wrong" mentality so he took his toys home and wouldn't let the other kids play with them anymore. Only a *toddler* should be allowed to demonstrate such egocentrism. Nothing in this world is completely black and white. Nobody has all the answers. If they think they do, then they are the most dangerous of all psychopaths or, at best, narcissistic, self-centered douchebags who shouldn't have their delusions entertained by anyone with rational thoughts.

Or they could be in the United States Congress.

Chapter 13

Along with all of my bible learnin', since I'd graduated from high school (and hated my grocery store job) it was finally time for me to enroll in classes at the Mansfield, Ohio branch of The Ohio State University. I'd taken six months off to save up some cash for tuition and books, so it was winter quarter when I started. Being the genius that I was, I scheduled my first class of the day at eight in the morning. So, whenever we were hit with serious snow I had to give myself practically two hours to get there. But bandmate and spiritual guru, James, was constantly loaning Christian rock cassettes to me so I had plenty new bands to investigate while driving.

BEGIN AWKWARDLY SPLICED IN RANT:

If you've never listened to Christian rock, most of the bands are incredibly lame rip-offs of whatever bands are/were huge in the secular world. There is always a lag between current trends in non-religious music and what's being plagiarized inside the Christian realm. For example, I converted in January of 1989 and most of the hair bands of the 80s were still huge. Motley Crue, Poison, Skid Row, Queensryche, and Ratt were dominating the pre-Grunge landscape. So, with the cultural lag, most Christian rock acts were still mimicking AC-DC, Iron Maiden and Judas Priest (check out X-Sinner, Barren Cross, Sacred Warrior, and Bloodgood for a few examples), who weren't remotely the red-hot bands at the time. Eventually holy hair band substitutes began appearing (White Cross, Holy Soldier, etc.) for Christians who missed their hairspray, spandex, and makeup. I don't lump Stryper in with these bands because they were on the ground floor of the hair band movement and actually had a sound of their own, if you don't count Michael Sweet's singing being quite similar to that dude in Styx. Of course there were plenty of Metallica (Deliverance) and Megadeth (Tourniquet) ripoffs as well for those who wanted to mosh gently and respectfully for the King of Kings.

You see, shortly after my conversion, James had convinced me that it wasn't healthy for a newborn in Christ to listen to secular bands; so we had a cassette burning ceremony in his backyard burn barrel. My entire collection (minus a couple that I "accidentally" left at home because I couldn't bear to part with them) of cock rock and thrash metal went up in flames. That may not seem very traumatic to envision, but music has always been incredibly vital to my existence. In fact, one of my favorite ways to emphasize this has always been to say, "Music is my oxygen! Without it, I'll die!" So purging my collection left a HUGE, gaping void in my life, and that meant I was at the mercy of the milquetoast-at-best Christian music industry to replace my beloved bands. For a few years, as a fledgling believer who rarely questioned anything he was told, I was able to subsist on this nutrient-deprived musical diet because I was brainwashed into accepting that these shoddy counterfeits were all I was allowed to listen to. Religion can truly lead a man to do some really stupid things and, to this day, I cringe while thinking of all the awesome tunes that went up in smoke in that barrel.

END RANT

Anyway, at college I was in a new and intimidating environment so I flew under the radar and didn't remotely advertise my faith. When I'd meet classmates for study sessions in the library, I'd fall into old habits like cursing in order to blend in with the crowd. Of course I'd beat myself up for it later while begging for forgiveness from the Lord (over and over again), a behavioral pattern that would only get worse with time.

*

But life at OSU wasn't all bad. One day I walked into the library's tiny lobby to grab a snack before my next class. Back then folks could smoke indoors (GASP!) and all the nursing students came to this area to smoke and bitch about their professors. Other students would plop on the little cushioned benches to snack, chat, and study. Before I could even get to the vending machines for my daily dose of Mountain Dew and Twix I heard a familiar voice call out, "Hey, Stephen! What's up, Stinky?"

It was Maddy, one of my best friends from high school. For some reason we called each other "Stinky" but I have no earthly idea how that started. It was a surprise to me that she was even in school at the branch (or The Twig, as students sarcastically called the tiny, three building campus) and she was definitely a sight for sore eyes. Finally, a familiar face! As we chatted a girl came out of the library and sat next to Maddy. At first I didn't pay much attention because I was so excited to catch up with my old friend, but when Maddy pointed to this young lady and said, "Stephen, this is Missy." I was mesmerized. Missy smiled and said hello, but it was obvious she was distracted. At the time I thought she was engrossed in thoughts of school but I later found out she'd just broken up with her boyfriend.

I didn't care if she wasn't locked in on my pasty white face. In fact, the only thing keeping me from stuttering and stumbling over my words was Missy's state of distraction. Sitting in front of me was the most gorgeous girl I had ever seen. She had short, curly, wine-red hair and stunning green eyes that sparkled with feisty attitude. For all I cared she could just continue not looking at me while rifling through her book bag because that allowed me to gape at her without appearing to be a creepy, mouth-breathing stalker.

Maddy and Missy had to excuse themselves and go to class so I was spared the opportunity to make a complete ass of myself. As they walked away, though, I couldn't help noticing that Missy looked just as amazing from the back. The little angel on my shoulder whispered that disciples of Jesus weren't supposed to notice tiny waists that ended in perfect, heart-shaped asses but I didn't care.

Good God! That chick was HOT!

When I got home that night, I called old Stinky up and begged her to get Missy's phone number. She agreed to and showed up promptly at my house the next day with the promised digits in hand. "She says she's never home because she works all the time," Maddy said, a frown creeping into the corners of her mouth. "But you can leave a message and she'll *try* to call you back."

WHOOSH!

All of my hopes for asking this girl out dropped to the floor like an Acme safe crushing Wile E. Coyote's skull. *Wow. She's never home and she works all the time. She'll try to call me back. That sounds promising. NOT!*

I did my best to forget that saucy siren named Missy by keeping myself busy with my studies at college and church but I never succeeded. In fact, I was in my British Literature class, struggling to understand *Beowulf* (in one of its earliest forms) when Missy walked by the open classroom door. She was all slicked up in a spicy black skirt/blouse ensemble (she taught ballroom dancing back then) and just seeing her glide past the doorway made my heart beat triple time. At first I seriously wondered if I was having a heart attack. Then, after calming down a little, I chided myself on getting that worked up over someone to whom I'd only said a few words. Sure she looked gorgeous enough to make me drool like Pavlov's dog, but what kind of a loser nearly pops an aorta over a girl he knows nothing about?

Clearly the answer to that question was: ME. Refocusing my brain on the professor's lecture after that was useless so I began formulating a plan to approach this mysterious hottie in the hallway after class. *I'll just go up to her and say, 'Hey, how's it* going? You see Maddy lately?' Nah, that'll sound like I really like Stinky. Hmmm...how about, 'You probably don't remember me, but my name's Stephen.'

No! That sounds pathetic and insecure, which I am, but she doesn't need to know that. Screw it! I'll just walk up to her and improvise. Yeah, because you're SO good at thinking on your feet, nerd boy! Yeah, but I've got God on my side now.

Lord, I prayed, please give me the courage to talk to Missy. I'm sorry I ogled her perfect rear end. I promise to never do that again if you will just help me speak to her. Okay, maybe not never but I'll do my best. In Jesus' name, Amen.

When the prof dismissed class I took a deep breath, stood, and puffed out my bony chest. The plan was to boldly march up to Missy in the hallway and just start speaking. God would guide my jittering jaws if I just had faith.

I walked out of the classroom numbly attempting to forge ahead to avoid overthinking things. So far so good. Sweet. Let's keep rolling. Okay, she went left so hopefully she's still in the hall instead of her next class. But, as soon as I turned the corner: BAM! There she was, sitting on a sofa chatting with friends. Her short, curly red hair covered one eye (which was strangely sexy to me) and her shapely, fishnet-clad legs were crossed as she smiled, laughed, and looked prettier than any girl I'd ever seen.

SCREEEEEECH!

My tennis shoes suddenly had impeccable brakes.

Oh no! My legs won't move! Lightning bolts of panic shot through my gut and my body began to shake with fright. *What am I DOING? I can't go up and talk to her! Are you kidding me? She'll laugh in my face!*

So I quickly spun on my heels and fled in the other direction, berating myself more with every step. *What am I DOING? I have this girl's phone number but I'm too much of a wuss to even talk to her? Come on, you pansy! Turn around and be a man! Where's your faith in God?*

I stopped, spun back around and began another shaky advance in Missy's direction, praying that I could fake some confidence until the Holy Ghost delivered it. *What are you DOING? She said she's never home and always busy but to leave a message and she MIGHT get back with me! It probably isn't even a real number. Screw this. I'm outta here!*

What choice did I have?

I bailed.

Retreated.

Fled the scene.

*

As I drove home that day, I grew angrier and angrier with myself with each passing mile, pummeling my Dodge Charger's steering wheel over and over with my palms. Obviously I was a failure with my new faith if I couldn't even trust God to give me the words to say to this girl!

Assuming that accepting Christ would undo years of shyness and lack of game with the ladies was quite naïve, yes, but I'd been told that God would transform me into a new creature. He could give me courage to face my fears. He would answer my prayers if I had faith.

This kind of thinking led me into a constant vicious cycle of praying, self-hatred (when my prayers weren't answered), more prayer (for help with my weaknesses), then more self-hatred. Discounting genetics' impact on my day-to-day reality while thinking that simply mumbling some words to the sky would change my situation is ridiculous to me now. I was born an introvert and will certainly die one. It's embarrassing to me now to admit that I once was ignorant enough to believe that a spiritual rebirth could fix this. Today I know there's nothing to be ashamed of because, as a famous bumper sticker asserts, I was born just fine the first time.

Chapter 14

By this time James and I had built up a solid band that was gradually developing a respectable set list of original tunes that were surprisingly good. This first incarnation of the band included:

Our drummer, Mark, was and still is a talented, perfectionist musician who's always been more like a brother to me than a first cousin. He was just starting to come into his own as a rocker who'd just started to grow his hair out from a respectable, small town Catholic boy length. Today he's a construction man who mostly plays guitar but the prick can play just about any instrument he lays his hands on. (Love you, Cuz!)

Gill, an incredibly intelligent, hyper, lanky, longhaired and talented guitarist, was employed at a printing factory at this time. Today he's a civil engineer in California. Gill is still the most talented riff writer I have ever jammed with. He could come up with the most insanely tasty chord progressions as easily as most people inhale and exhale.

Gill's cousin Darren, a mulleted, happy-go-lucky dude who overachieved at flatulence, was our rhythm guitarist. Darren was very talented and rock solid as a rhythm player, which is also uncommon. After serving in Iraq, Darren is now employed as a machinist and still lives in Ohio.

And finally there was our loveable, longhaired goofball vocalist, Dave, who was slightly older than James, which made him the geezer of the group. He worked in a foam factory at the time. His voice was often compared to Ozzy Osbourne's and Yes' Jon Anderson. Dave drove an amazing white van (all passengers were required to autograph the interior with a Sharpie) that had bullhorns on the hood and a cow tail dangling from the rear doors. This rustbucket also had a PA speaker mounted in the front grill that enabled Dave to broadcast hilarious comments to pedestrians and motorists via a CB microphone. Today he works in an Ohio factory and records epic jams in his basement.

*

Now we had a complete group with decent songwriting chemistry but the only problem was we didn't have a name. Every time I'd tell someone how excited I was about this new, best band I'd ever been in they'd ask, "What's the name?"

"Uh," I'd stammer. "Well, we, uh, we don't have a name yet." Even if you don't know squat about marketing it's obvious that the lack of even a shitty name can really put a damper on a band getting somewhere. Every single person who heard this reply from me immediately lost all interest and never asked again.

So James and I sat on his sofa one night brainstorming metal monikers that would both inspire the masses to headbang and assure them that we were thumpers of the Bible as well. Oh how I wish I could remember the glorious list of names that *didn't* make the grade because the oh-so-brilliant one we agreed on was...

Drum roll...

HOLY SHIELD!

Yep. That's right: Holy Shield.

Sound like any other exclamation in the English language you've ever heard?

Sigh.

That'd be the one.

It was supposed to be a reference to the Armor of God (Ephesians 6:10-18) but instead it sounded like we were cursing about excrement. Thankfully our lead guitarist didn't tolerate the name for long. "BULL!" Gill stomped his foot and slapped his knee, his usual gesture while calling bullshit about something. "We can't use that name! Are you *crazy*?"

"Why not?" I asked, clueless as usual.

Gill's eyes bugged out in disbelief. "Why *not*? Because it sounds like something else...something that we're not supposed to say."

"Um, I'm still not getting it. What's it sound like?"

"Are you KIDDING me? Listen to it: HOLY SHIELD!" He paused, mouth open and curly locks swinging from the emphasis he'd put on the phrase.

My head cocked to the side like a baffled basset hound. "What? You're just saying Holy Shield. So?"

Nearly exploding into orbit, Gill screamed, "Oh my...GOSH! Can't you hear it? Holy shi--"

"OH!"

"Yeah, no way I'm playin' in a band with *that* name!" Darren added.

Even though he got the double entendre, after Gill pointed it out *once* at a band meeting, James still had trouble letting go of the name. It was *his* brainchild and he always held onto those like a pit-bull clamps onto an intruder's femur. Eventually we accepted James' second (and much better) idea for a name: Critical Dispatch. Even though a sticker James stumbled upon at his factory job inspired this name it was chosen because it sounded cool and clearly (or so we thought) indicated our evangelistic agenda.

*

Around this time I was sitting in a hallway at OSU with my feet propped up on the chair beside me, attempting to slog through the original text of *Beowulf*, when someone kicked my feet onto the floor. Who so rudely jolted me out of my studies? It was that hot chick, Missy, whose phone number I'd had but not used.

As I gaped and blinked my bleary, beady eyes at her, she plopped down on the chair beside me and said, "You've had my number for two weeks. Are you gonna call me or what?"

Within days, after talking on the phone several times (about everything but my born again status) we had our first date. I remember desperately trying to think of an original activity for the occasion but failing in grand fashion. *We can't just do to dinner and a movie! That's so cliché! This chick is WAY out of my league. She'll know how boring I am!* In the end I was so paralyzed by fear of screwing this first date up that I gave up and asked Missy what she'd like to do. To my great relief she just shrugged and said, "How about dinner and a movie?"

Whew! Off the hook!

So we met at the mall and window-shopped for a while before our movie, *Three Amigos*, started. The whole date was a blur (*Please don't let her think I'm an idiot!* was my mantra) for me but Missy remembers it in great detail. She always says that, at first, she thought I had the personality of a doorknob, but I won her over by playing with and petting kittens in a pet store. At the time I thought I hated cats but loved dogs, so I'm sure I just did it to impress a gorgeous redhead. Hell, I would've cuddled a crocodile that was gnawing my hand off if it meant a second date with her!

After the movie we grabbed some dinner then sat in my car awkwardly trying to get to know one another. No matter what topic came up, I was petrified that Missy would ask if I was religious. She knew that I had long hair and played bass in a rock band, but there was no way I was going to risk scaring her away. I was already demonstrating my social ineptitude enough as it was so, to score some cool points, I popped a Guns n' Roses *Appetite for Destruction* cassette into the stereo and proceeded to gush about how much they (not Jesus) had changed my life.

In the end, Missy asked for a goodnight kiss which (HALLELUJAH!) went very well and another date was scheduled. As I drove home I recall being tempted to beat myself up for not mentioning Christ just to impress a girl. I'd already had it beaten into my head that, at every opportunity, it was mandatory to somehow allude to my faith. Any failure to proselytize was supposedly equivalent to Peter denying Christ by the burn barrel. Thankfully, the combination of being new to Christian brainwashing combined with the hormonal rush of getting to kiss a gorgeous girl kept me from succumbing to anything but pure joy and excitement.

Of course, that would change quite quickly.

Here's little ole me on the day of my
Catholic confirmation
(April 1981); It had nothing to do
with *Star Wars*, motherfuckers!

Behold the uber-nerdy, stealth
atheist, circa 1984.

1987: Still an atheist, still a geek
beginning to sprout a mullet!

Our engagement picture (1989): We're smiling because the love of Jeebus is in our hearts

At a comic con (2013): Sans Jesus and closer than ever because of it

Critical Dispatch: We were the champions...of the world...er, the talent show!

From left to right: My first recording session at Sleeping Giant Studios; C.D.'s first big gig at Willard High School; Me attempting to out-glam Poison

The interior band photo for the *Fate of the Wicked* E.P.

This is the face of a naïve, first year teacher who's about to have a
showdown with an anxiety disorder (1998)

An older, wiser, rock n' roller cleverly disguised as a responsible
adult.

Chapter 15

Soon Critical Dispatch was playing its first gig, for a youth group in Shelby, Ohio, thanks to Dave living in that town at the time. For weeks and weeks we rehearsed our butts off and whipped up a strong forty-five minute set of homemade, messianic metal anthems, including such Top 40 hits as: "Flight 777" (a cheesy number about going to heaven which began with a keyboard simulation of an airplane taking off) and "The Mask" (which started with a drum and bass section blatantly plagiarized from Ozzy's "Crazy Train"). We were sounding tighter than a ten-pound rat stuffed into a five-pound bag. All of our guitars had fresh strings. Mark had new sticks as well as heads on his drums. And James, well, he had the same keyboards as always but he was pumped. Dave? Well, Dave was the same cool, calm, and demented guy he always was.

And me?

I was full-on pants-crappingly terrified about the show. Why? Because every other show I'd done as a bassist had been played with the aid of the world's most common anti-anxiety medication: booze. Most of the gigs I'd had in the past were either for high school graduation parties (free beer!) or in bars (chug beer before the show due to being underage!) so playing in a church for a youth group with nothing to chug but water had me as antsy as a politician hooked up to a lie detector. Luckily I talked it out with my bandmates and they prayed with and for me so, come gig time, I was as cool as a cucumber.

WRONG!

Even though the audience at the First Church of God contained about thirty people, this pasty white bass player was practically soiling his tighty whities during the first three or four songs. After that my nerves settled down and I had a blast. As a band we were raw and unprofessional but the kids in that youth group ate it up. They were so desperate for something heavier than praise and worship music that they didn't mind this group of awkward, nervous misfits with no PA (only a microphone connected to the church's speakers) who had to apologize for their drummer's EXTREMELY squeaky drum throne that nearly drowned out their instruments.

*

So we chalked gig number one up as a roaring success. This gave us confidence to book other shows and somehow we landed a spot at a festival in downtown Mansfield, Ohio. By this time we'd added a couple new tunes to our repertoire: "Just a Game" featured Dave's lyrical warning about the dangers of using Ouija boards (and a sweet breakdown bass riff that I wrote, my first real musical contribution to the group); and "Prison of Addiction", which was ironically written by James, who, like Gill and Darren, smoked like a chimney.

For this second concert we decided to amp our rock star apparel to look more professional. It was still the eighties so bands dressing in typical street clothes were frowned upon. We didn't go all out, but I remember wearing some fashionably ripped jeans and going a little wilder with the hairspray on the top of my glorious mullet. James was just starting to grow his hair out, which was really starting to clash with his seventies porn star mustache.

*

Since we'd been dating for a while and I was still attempting to convince her that I was a studly, four string slingin' rocker, I invited Missy to the show. She immediately promised to come which, on one hand was great but, on the other hand, sucked because it was now imperative that I come out of the Jesus Closet.

How will she react? I mean, those parties she's taken me to have been full of nothing but drinking, dirty jokes, and secular metal. Plus, she cusses like a trucker. Will she pretend to be cool with my faith then stop returning my calls? Will she laugh in my face? Calm down! She'll probably just freak a little then calm down and accept it.

No. She'll DEFINITELY laugh in my face, then run!

*

Finally, when it was almost gig time, I steeled my nerves for the big reveal. Missy had asked me to come to her house and hang out before our date, so I had an hour of driving time to build my confidence with nonstop pep talks and prayers. *Lord Jesus, I don't want to let You down. Please give me the strength to profess my faith today. I know I'm weak and still a newborn in Christ, but all I want is to make You happy.*

When I arrived, Missy had left the door unlocked with a note explaining that she was in the shower. So I let myself in and sat (sweating it out) on the sofa. Finally, she shuffled sleepily into the room, hair still wet, and collapsed on the sofa with me. After we'd snuggled and chatted for a while I finally had to come out with it.

"Um...there's something I have to tell you," I squeaked, having a hard time hearing my own voice over the nervous hammering of my heart.

Lifting her head off my shoulder, Missy groggily asked, "Yeah? What's that?"

Here it goes. It's now or never! "The band I'm in...it's a Christian rock band. I'm a born-again Christian." *Oh, man. Here comes the "I don't think we should see each other any more but we can still be friends" speech.*

"Oh," Missy calmly replied. "So am I."

"Cool!" I half-heartedly exclaimed, thinking of all the F-bombs she'd dropped and beers she'd gulped. *Is she just saying this to be polite? Or is she pretending to be a Christian because she likes me?* "I mean, don't think I'm, like, all uptight about it and everything. I just believe in God and try to live for Him."

"So do I," she said, snuggling back down onto my shoulder.

Based on what I'd observed so far in our brief time as a couple, I was very skeptical about Missy's sincerity. How could she act the way that she acted yet be saved? Don't get me wrong, I wanted to believe her with every fiber of my being because I was already falling in love with her, but I also didn't want to stray from the Christian path. I mean, James had warned me not to date unbelievers. He'd seen too many of his friends backslide from trying to fit in with their heathen hottie girlfriends. And I'd already nursed a few beers at the parties Missy had taken me to so I wouldn't be the odd duck out.

So, as we were lying there on that sofa together, I resolved to reign in my emotions while sitting back to see just how committed to Christ my girlfriend was. If she started to walk the walk more then I'd stay in the relationship. If not, then I'd just have to break up with her. Once I had that settled, my swirling, anxious thoughts settled into a peaceful, contented flow again.

Of course, I took this as God giving me His seal of approval for choosing obedience to Him over an earthly love. Never mind the fact that I was being a completely hypocritical asswipe who was barely acting a tad bit more religious than Missy was. Looking back on that self-righteous resolution fills me with both remorse and gratitude. There I was dating an intelligent, sexy young lady while smugly thinking I had some kind of moral high ground to look down on her from.

And how much would I have regretted choosing to break up with her, thus losing the love of my life, in the interest of pursuing a relationship with a fictional deity?

It boggles the mind.

Chapter 16

There isn't much that stands out in my memory about the Mansfield gig, other than playing in an outdoor band shell to a tiny, polite audience of (maybe) twenty people. My parents were in attendance, despite their reservations about my relatively new religious phase; Dad was impressed that I was finally in a band with a singer who could actually hold a note. I also remember James being angry with Dave for using cheat sheets because he didn't have the lyrics memorized. Oh, and after the show, Missy introduced me to the joy of authentic Greek gyros. Drool!

After this we played (for free) a very unremarkable party in James' sister-in-law's boyfriend's garage and another at a big backyard shindig that Dave's friend had. Following these incredibly glamorous shows, Mark, also known as Fudd, began losing interest in the project. He really wasn't all that into the whole born again thing anyway. So he simply stopped showing up for band practices, which really pissed all of us off. We kept calling him and reminding him when the next practice was but he persisted in staying AWOL. Gill, who lived in the same little village of New Washington, Ohio, reported seeing our wayward drummer associating with some *sinners* of the worst sort: the local drinkers and druggies, to be exact.

We all prayed earnestly for him, hoping that Jesus would show the Fuddster the error of his boozing ways. Of course we were all operating on the assumption that, because he was fraternizing with these guys, then he *must* be up to all sorts of hedonism. We had zero eyewitnesses' testimonies for proof but rushed to judgment anyway. Granted, I called Mark while writing this chapter and he chuckled, confirming that he was indeed partaking in quite a few substances at the time.

Eventually we asked Mark to meet us at his local Dairy Queen to talk. Our whole self-righteous crew piled into Dave's van and headed off to sever an offending limb from the Critical Dispatch body. Gill (a high school classmate of Mark's) and I felt the most awkward about it. Dave wasn't exactly thrilled with our zeal in the matter but he was such an easygoing dude that he never liked making waves.

When we got there, poor Mark was sitting on the steps of the village's tiny band shell adjacent to the Dairy Queen. His body language indicated that he knew the axe was about to fall but he put on a brave face. We all sat down on the steps with him and James lead the way as the bad cop, with the rest of us filling the good cop roles. Still, it was an ugly five against one ambush masked with a lot of good, old-fashioned Christian politeness. After a lot of Salem Witch Hunt style interrogation from us and mostly guilty, downcast grunts from Fudd, he still didn't admit to partying with his buddies but, in the end, we informed him that we were moving on to find a new drummer. Of course, we assured him, our oh-so-holy prayers for his backslidden state would continue.

Mark told me later that it was mostly a relief to get the inevitable confrontation over with. He knew he didn't want to be in the band but didn't have the heart to tell us. The only real guilt he felt wasn't from our browbeating and sermonizing. The work ethic his family had instilled in him ensured that, if work had been committed to, he felt honor-bound to perform it. He hadn't bowed out of the situation and wasn't fulfilling his role; that's where his remorse originated, not the so-called conviction of the Holy Spirit.

Now, should a band give a non-contributing member the boot after several fair chances? Absolutely. And we did that. What bothers me about this event was the moral judgment that occurred. All of us were gossiping about Mark behind his back but assuring each other that what we were doing was simply expressing wholesome, Christlike concern for a comrade. We weren't talking about a struggling friend behind his back. We were relaying prayer requests.

Were any of us perfect?

Hell no!

Were any of us participating in sinful behavior at that time?

Absolutely!

Would any of us been righteously indignant if we found out the other guys were blabbing about our personal struggles when we weren't around?

Hmmm...let me see...

FUCK YEAH!

It's been said that Christianity is the only army that shoots its wounded, and it's true. I'm not saying that gossiping and judgment don't occur in the secular realm but most churches seem to excel in both categories. Our six man band was a microcosm of the church itself and this incident with Mark was, sadly, just one of many escalating examples of our self-righteousness.

The Bible teaches the faithful to both avoid judging others (Jesus' commandment) and also to separate themselves from unbelievers (Paul's commandment). According to the New Testament Jesus hung out with prostitutes and other sinners without behaving like or condemning them, yet Paul's hardass epistles browbeat the church for tolerating any association with such folk.

So which is the proper course of action? Do these contradictory messages within the Good Book tend to freeze people into a state of inaction, causing excessively judgmental lip flapping about the church's wounded? Do Paul's militant commands lead Christians to constantly turn/tattle on one another like snippy little school children? Or does the stagnant, insular culture of the church shelter its members, thus leading to a state of arrested emotional development, leading to perpetually immature, high school drama?

My money's on that last theory.

Over the years I've noticed that many "sold out" believers become so naïve and pampered from avoiding the secular (i.e. anything that forces them to face both the random beauty and hideousness of human existence) that they can't handle reality very well. If a book, movie or song offends them then it must be banned or burned! If someone curses in front of them they twitch and cringe as if doomsday has arrived and demand that their ears' virginal status be respected. If such behavior isn't the epitome of childishness then I don't know what is.

If you don't agree with me, try taking any of those situations and plugging them into a toddler's daily life scenario and see what you get. For example: Little Jonny is playing happily in his backyard sandbox with his friend Loretta Lou. While they're driving toy cars across the dusty terrain Loretta begins singing, "Girls Rule and Boys Drool" (a song she heard on TV). Jonny finds this offensive and demands that she stop. Loretta ignores him. She has rights too, ya know! Jonny, being the egocentric little snotrocket that he is, cannot comprehend that, if this song bothers *him*, that it might not offend everybody else in the world. "Stop singing that stupid song, Loretta!" He orders for the second time.

Loretta, spurred on by the obvious irritation that she's accidentally caused, begins to sing with even more gusto. "Oh-oh, boys are stinky doodie heads/Boys poop and pee their beds!"

At this point Little Jonny loses his shit, jumps to his feet, points imperiously at Loretta, and screams, "I told you to STOP it! You get outta *my* sandbox. It's *mine* and you can't play in it no more!"

Sound familiar?

Exactly.

Chapter 17

After succeeding in casting out the unbeliever we, of course, immediately pursued a tried and true Christian drummer to replace him, right?

EL WRONGO!

At our first post-firing-of-Mark meeting, James asked if any of us knew any drummers. The only good one I knew (a guy I'd been in secular bands with--we'll call him Tom) wasn't a believer so he was out. So we advertised and had auditions. Well, to be more accurate, I should call them "trainwrecks" because literally every dillhole who showed up couldn't keep a beat to save his ass. And then there were the (sadly) typical, shiftless hobo musicians who were good but either had no transportation (still living in Mommy's basement, jobless, and addicted to videogames) or no drum kit to play. Seriously, I can understand being down on your luck and having to sell your beloved instrument to pay the rent, but why the hell would you attempt to audition for a band with no fucking instrument?

Weeks and weeks of spinning our wheels in Percussion Purgatory brought us back to considering my heathen friend Tom. I don't remember if it was my idea or James', but we decided to have him come over to jam. If there was musical chemistry there, we were going to pour on the evangelical sales pitch and pray the devil right out of his scrawny ass.

This practice became a sickeningly sinister method that we'd use to replace departing members throughout most of the band's existence. Of course we rationalized that God was using us to save these wayward metalheads, so the ends justified the means. Never mind the fact that we'd have to babysit spiritual newborns who would constantly put us in embarrassing situations by "stumbling in their walks with Christ". What was important was improving as a band so we could become Christian rock stars...er, I mean, rescuing folks from the pits of Hell!

So Tom came over to jam and kicked total ass. He drummed up some metal magic and threw in some amazingly tasty, Jazz-influenced fills for good measure. I was able to lock in with him instantly because we'd already been in a million bands together. Those of us already in the band (mostly) kept our poker faces engaged until he left but, as soon as his truck pulled out of James' driveway, we were giggling and high-fiving like giddy school girls who'd just met their favorite boy band.

"Dude!" Darren exclaimed. "I don't want to get ahead of ourselves here, but Tom freakin' rocks! Holy cow!"

"I know!" Gill added. "Holy crap! Did you hear that double bass?"

Smiling like the proverbial porker rolling in feces, I gloated, "Told ya. Tom kicks a--uh, butt, doesn't he?"

And thus the *completely selfless* conversion of Tom V. was initiated. Within no time at all he was accepting Jesus into his drumstick twirling heart and Critical Dispatch was creating killer tunes that were light years ahead of our initial efforts. And none of us could wipe the grins from our self-righteous faces.

We were on our way, baby!

Chapter 18

Meanwhile, back on the church front, it didn't take long for me to become bored with the Naz. I didn't even realize how bored I was until James invited me to go with him, and his wife, to a non-denominational assembly in Fremont, OH called Victory Christian Fellowship (VCF). At first, the fifty-minute drive to this church was discouraging. I knew my parents would have a cow about me driving that far, in addition to five days a week of hauling my pasty hide to college, but I thought I'd humor James and ride along. *A church is a church*, I thought. *Sure the Naz isn't exactly pulse-pounding, but it's still light years more interesting than mass! James just thinks VCF rules because he wasn't raised Catholic.*

But, as soon as we walked in the front door I knew that VCF was an entirely different planet from Nazereneville. Gaping like a buffoon, I followed Mr. and Mrs. James through the lobby door, a pleasing potpourri breeze (common to all fine nondenominational establishments, including but not limited to: bookstores, sanctuaries, concert venues, etc.) washed over me and there were ushers in suits greeting us with programs while warmly exclaiming, "God bless you! So glad to see you today."

Even though this professional greeting was quite genuine and impressive, the music booming from the sanctuary, along with a palpable buzz of excitement in the air, practically sucked me into the building. This was no funeral dirge, Catholic organ music! Nor was it the we're-not-quite-as-depressing-as-those-damn-mackerel-snappers Nazarene organ music. This...this was damn near rock n' roll praise and worship music!

Lassoed by this auditory bliss, I practically stiff-armed anyone in my path while swerving through the teeming crowd. *Get the hel—heck outta my way! I must confirm that this isn't a hallucination!* There was simply no way that this church could possibly have non-turdy tunes. EVERY church did, well, at least every non-black church. Clearly there was a passage in the Bible somewhere that required songs of suckitude for the entire Caucasian persuasion: "Thou shalt flagellate the porcelain ears of thine flock until the congregation weepeth for mercy." (Psalms Pt. 2: The Sequel)

After several agonizing minutes of slithering through the squirming masses, I found a vantage point that enabled me to see the band. Instantly the clouds parted and the Holy Ghost descended upon my mulleted head while choirs of angels harmonized in Heaven. Why? Because, up there on that stage, behind that sleek, glass pulpit, was a complete rock band. I'm talking electric, acoustic and bass guitars, drums, keyboards, and a horn section! Luckily James and his wife had followed me, smirking at my gaping tourist face, because my buns had already planted themselves firmly on the closest chair, not that sitting with strangers would've even mattered at that point.

After the usual church business of announcements and special songs was briskly taken care of, the uber-charismatic Pastor Scott sprinted onstage to pilot the pulpit. Now, the sermons at the Naz were never horrible, but they certainly were never fascinating or challenging. I'm fairly certain that, if Pastor Mike had dared to regale his congregation with such fare, he'd have been hauled before a council of crusty old deacons and ridden out on a rail. It wasn't that he sucked at his job; he was simply operating within the acceptable parameters of his situation.

So, as soon as Pastor Scott launched into his passionate, intellectually challenging message that twisted my brain into a gray matter pretzel, complete with hilarious and engaging humor, I was hooked like a junkie after his first taste of Smack. There wasn't a single don't-rock-the-boat bone in this preacher's body. He challenged people to examine the scriptures in the original Greek and Hebrew. He also, as I'd find out later, urged his flock to follow their own hearts on issues that the Bible wasn't explicit about. When it came time for the collection plates to circulate, Pastor Scott didn't whine and beg like a pitiful Beagle looking for table scraps. He cheerfully and confidently reminded everyone of their responsibilities and the blessings that would return to all faithful tithers.

By the time we exited VCF, I was begging James and his wife to let me ride with them on the following Sunday. They chuckled and said it would be no problem. *Finally*, I thought. *I've found my church home! Just wait 'til I show this place to Missy. She's gonna LOVE it!*

*

Sure enough, Missy was similarly impressed and we began consistently tagging along to services at VCF. As a result, we both became more and more committed in our faith and felt that we were growing spiritually. We prayed together, read scripture together, and had deep conversations about our beliefs.

Of course, my parents still pitched a bitch about us traveling almost an hour each week. "Why can't you find a church here in town? Or at least one a helluva lot closer than Fremont?" my mother growled.

"Because VCF is the COOLEST church I've ever seen, Mom! Besides, I'm not driving. James is."

"Still! That's just ridiculous going all that way when there's a church on every damn block right here in Willard."

Of course I wrote off her angst as mere pissyness over my non-practicing Catholic status, which it was, but Dad snarled about it as well. "You'd better not think you're driving MY car all the way to Fremont, not when you're racking up miles going to college and your *girlfriend's* house all the damn time!"

"But I'm *not* driving, Dad. James is. I just chip in for the gas money."

"Yeah, well, if I find out you're driving MY car up there then *your* ass is in trouble! And you'd better not be handing over your money to that place, either!"

"I won't. Gosh!"

*

A few weeks into our VCF pilgrimages, James pulled me aside at band practice to inform me that Missy and I could hitch a ride *every once in a while*, but our mooching ways were no longer going to be tolerated. If we wanted to attend Victory Christian Fellowship then we needed to start driving our freeloading behinds to Fremont.

Outwardly I pretended that this was all fine and dandy, but this hurt my feelings quite a bit. How was this mooching? James was already driving there anyway and there were empty seats in his car, right? We gave him gas money. So why was it un-Christian of him to help a brother out? For all the times (and in

Critical Dispatch there were quite a few) I'd had the "Is that something Jesus would do?" line leveled at me to curtail my sinful, selfish ways, why didn't it apply to James? Apparently helping a brother achieve maximum spiritual enlightenment while avoiding the wrath of his heathen parents was entirely too much to ask.

Interesting!

When I made the mistake of confiding in one of the other band members about feeling slighted, my trust was promptly betrayed, which resulted in another lecture from James about supposedly being a freeloading deadbeat.

So, what lesson did I learn? Bumming a ride to church was an unholy nuisance, and tattling, backstabbing and hypocrisy were standard operating procedure in the Body of Christ.

Duly noted!

*

Now that we were spurned sponges, Missy and I talked it over and decided to take turns driving to Fremont on Sundays. Looking back, this was one of many early instances of our blossoming ability to communicate and compromise as a couple. We'd also agreed to pay for our own food on dates whenever money was too tight.

Of course, whenever it was my turn to drive to VCF, I had to lie to my parents ("I'm driving up to James' house to ride with him to church.") and deal with a guilty conscience on top of my resentment toward James. In retrospect, Dad had to have been checking the car's odometer so he knew his pious, preachy son was taking creative liberties with the facts.

WWJD, right?

During the time we were active members at VCF, we learned quite a bit. Some of it was a bit out there, though. I remember one sermon in which Pastor Scott, relying heavily on his *Dake's Annotated Reference Bible*, taught about an epoch of civilization on earth that was destroyed before Adam and Eve were created. Supposedly, if you dig deeply into the original Hebrew texts, the angel Lucifer ruled over a Pre-Adamite (the human race version 1.0) paradise that was ruined when God's favorite angel's pride caused him to lead a revolt against the Most High. This sermon held my imagination spellbound for months on end.

In the meantime, if you, dear reader, could use some cheap entertainment, Google the phrase "Pre-Adamite". Even the most jaded, pessimistic eyes will be surprised by the sheer madness attached to this theory. Christians over the years have used this interpretation of the Bible to rationalize everything from racism (All non-whites are inferior because only Adam's spawn were created in God's image, not them there Negros and

Asians!) to evolution (We can explain why those pesky evolutionists got SOME facts right! Dinosaur bones are left over from the Pre-Adamite era.). Back then, Pastor Scott's glowing praise for the *Dake's Bible* convinced me to purchase my own copy. I dug into that sucker and highlighted the bejesus out of it. The supposed layers of meaning in scripture that were lost in translation fascinated me, to say the least. What hidden gems could be unearthed by consulting experts on Hebrew and Greek? How many divine truths were being obscured by inept translators or the limitations of the English language?

It never occurred to me to question how an omnipotent God who wanted to clearly communicate His infallible Word could possibly, in good conscience, allow shitty linguists or human frailties to get in the way. I mean, the Bible claims He doesn't want anyone to burn forever in Hell, so how could He damn someone to Hell because King James' translators sucked at their jobs? In what universe is it fair to burn people for eternity due to a holy book's translations and modifications that were obviously influenced by human agendas, both personal and political? If God really is omnipotent and omniscient, shouldn't He be the ONLY one capable of perfect communication that even a human filter couldn't fuck up?

Ironically, this intense study of Dake's annotations led to some unsavory discoveries which in turn caused me to (along with the fear of parental punishment over the miles accumulating on Dad's car) reevaluate my VCF attendance. What unsavory discoveries, you ask? Well, along with that fruity Pre-Adamite nonsense, Dake's also included some notes that condemned interracial relationships and hinted that Caucasians were the bee's knees, all according to God's holy Word, of course!

Still, we received some impeccable instruction about marriage at VCF. Missy and I got engaged on July 4, 1989 after dating for a grand total of six months. Of course, everyone in our families was really excited about this, well, except for my mom who worried that we were too young and rushing things. Still, even though she was worried, she did a great job of not pouncing on us with sermons and lectures. She did ask if Missy was on birth control, though. My pious response was, "Mom! Christians don't have premarital sex!" For some reason Mom was quite skeptical.

So Missy and I attended VCF's month-long seminar for engaged couples and married folks, examining what the Bible has to say about getting hitched. Pastor Scott did an amazing job of teaching us about gender differences and how they affect communication, emotions, and every other facet of relationships. If you've ever read *Men Are From Mars and Women Are From Venus* then you know what we learned, in a nutshell. To people who'd had the benefit of top notch pre-marital/marital counseling it probably wasn't groundbreaking stuff, but at least it was being taught by a man who was still on his first marriage, unlike that John Gray guy. Pastor Scott even tackled ticklish topics like foreplay and oral sex. All the faithful in the sanctuary were excited to hear that there are no scriptures forbidding fellatio or cunnilingus, so we were encouraged to pray about it and follow our hearts. Surprisingly, every dude in the congregation didn't storm the pulpit to high five Pastor Scott that day.

I mean, seriously. Very few preachers have the balls to teach that info.

Chapter 19

Flushed with zeal induced by Critical Dispatch's newfound musical kickassery, James soon became convinced that we needed to purchase our own PA system. Of course we'd made absolutely no money for the few shows we'd played (almost everyone who wanted us to play expected us to play for free; more on that later). Over the course of several band meetings we were persuaded to take out a loan together, splitting the payments six ways. At first I (along with Darren and Tom) was pretty iffy on the idea. Here I was making peon wages in a grocery store while attempting to pay my own way through college while Darren was a lowly underling mowing lawns for a landscaping company and Tom delivered pizzas. Yet we were going to be expected to fork over the same amount as three guys with sweet factory paychecks?

Of course, James had a real knack for persuasion. He was a firm believer that we'd make God look bad by doing anything half-assed (i.e. within our budget), even if that meant going into debt. The Bible doesn't have anything negative to say about borrowing money, right? Proverbs 22:7 ("The rich rule over the poor, and the borrower is slave to the lender.") is always misinterpreted!

I may have been a young Christian but I was quickly learning from my peers the fine art of cherry picking which verses to follow and which to ignore.

Hint: *It all depends on your personal biases and the situation. Don't let any believer tell you that Biblical morals ain't relative.*

*

Eventually James even bulldozed us into taking out a loan for an RV (for all of those *epic* tours we booked) and coughing up money to rent rehearsal space (because the cops kept getting called to his house due to our excessive volume; these go to eleven!) as well. Any time we'd balk at the expenses, he'd whip out some material he'd gleaned from various prosperity preachers. These oh-so biblically accurate theologians preached that Jesus was indeed wealthy during his ministry, so it was important to name anything you wanted, claim it in the name of Jesus, and then wait for God to deliver it. Or, as critics of this philosophy dubbed it: Name it, claim it, fake it, take it.

Let this be a lesson to any rockers who're reading this: starting a band on a foundation of debt is a HORRIBLE IDEA! I don't care what kind of awesome creative chemistry you have. The stress from the debt will rip the group apart and cause all kinds of animosity.

Want some more proof?

*

As soon as the PA loan was a go for Critical Dispatch, Dave, our lead singer, announced that he was leaving the band. Yep, our loyal human Golden Retriever with the Ozzy pipes was done. He was in the band for fun and felt that the rest of us were getting way more serious about things than he was. It was like a dating relationship that was going entirely too fast. Here we were having a good time as a couple when all of a sudden the girlfriend wants him to settle down and join her in the unholy acrimony of debt.

Woah there, Sparkles!

Too fast too soon!

Of course, all of us were suckerpunched by this news, but I took it especially hard. I pretty much worshipped Dave. His quirky sense of humor and eccentric, easygoing ways were like a soothing balm to me. He had become quite a mentor. There were many nights when I'd stay up almost all night at Dave's house just marinating in his peaceful, former-stoner genius. One minute we'd be acting stupid and shooting a homemade potato cannon and the next we were having deep philosophical discussions about spiritual issues. Many times we'd end up recording ourselves on his reel-to-reel four-track machine, reversing the reels, listening to what our voices sounded like backwards, then memorizing the gibberish so we could record ourselves speaking backwards and playing it backwards to see if it was decipherable. The whole time during this process we would be giggling insanely and shushing each other out of fear of waking Dave's wife. Better times without the enhancement of pharmaceuticals cannot be had, my friends. Maybe he wasn't perfect, but he'll always be proof to me that all Christians aren't self-righteous assholes.

I came home from practice on the night Dave announced his retirement, called Missy, and immediately began blubbering like a baby before I could even spit out the news. It was about as heartbreaking as finding out that the vet had to put down your favorite pooch, sure, but weeping on the phone to my new fiancé was quite embarrassing. But, did that shame enable me to put a stopper on the wheezing, snot-bubbling tear fest that was erupting from my soul? HELL no!

Fortunately for me, Missy was/is a very understanding lass. She probably just assumed that I was Emo before Emo even existed. Or that I was barely hetero, which I've been accused of several times. Either way, I'm thankful that she didn't call me a whiney bitch, hang up, and move on to a more *manly* man, whatever that is.

*

So there we were, lead singerless with the ink still wet on our PA loan's paperwork. Now five of us had to carry the debt load, but several of us were so strapped that more blood couldn't be squeezed from our turnips. The three band members with lucrative factory jobs had to split up Dave's payment amongst each other. None of them were happy about it, but it was our only option. We'd made our bed and had to lie in it.

And then there was the little matter of finding a new vocalist. If you've never been in a band then let me assure you that finding a good singer (who isn't completely psychotic) is about as easy as finding a virgin working in a whorehouse. Multiply those shitty odds by the Christian only (in a hick town area) factor and, well, you get the picture. We put ads up everywhere. Many well-meaning folks auditioned but most were so tone deaf that James' neighbors (and households within a twenty mile radius) complained that their dogs were attempting suicide and milk was curdling in their refrigerators. The few singers who *could* carry a tune had choirboy voices that totally did not mix well with metal music.

Soon it became time to broaden our search in the hopes that a great singer might be willing to drive up to one hundred miles to be our frontman. We drove down to Columbus, OH and passed out flyers at our favorite Christian rock concert venue: The King's Place. There were several interesting nibbles on our line from that endeavor (including a guy with amazing, power metal pipes who *humbly* called himself Justin Time and another guy who screamed so hard in his audition that he gave himself a vomiting migraine fit) but nothing panned out.

Needless to say, our morale was sinking fast. Just when we'd started to hit our stride with songwriting and musicianship now we couldn't book gigs without a singer. Still, we soldiered on, composing songs that were more melodic, slicker, and heavier than anything we'd written thus far. Our songwriting chemistry was so intense at this point that we'd play the same tunes over and over, perfecting them as we went without getting tired of them. We ended almost every practice with face-eclipsing grins. All of us could just *feel* that something special was happening and that sent electric thrills through our guts. Even a deaf man could tell that we were on to something.

Now if only we could find a FREAKING SINGER!

Chapter 20

Eventually the guilt and stress over lying about driving the long distance to Fremont led to a search for a church like VCF that was close by. So Missy and I began pew hopping. As usual, most of the churches were painfully boring and stuffy. But then I remembered that we'd been invited to check out a church that had just started by Jose and Hilda Arroyo, the owners of our local Christian bookstore.

Jose was this stocky, larger than life Latino who'd been quite a boozer and brawler in his youth. He had tons of tattoos, which endeared him to me, and his boisterous enthusiasm for all things Jehovah was infectious. There were many mornings that I stopped by to shop and chat after a long night on third shift and Jose never failed to light my spiritual fuse. If he could pump me up just by talking to me in his tiny bookstore, his church had to be cool, right?

But, before I attended my first service at The Prophet's Guild, as Jose and Hilda's church was called, I consulted with James. Even though he had eroded my trust (over the ride mooching incident) a bit, I still valued his opinion at that point. He encouraged me to go ahead and check the place out, but he warned me that he knew some loyal attendees who were "weirdoes and freaks". Apparently he'd experienced these oddballs at other churches and they were the type of Christian one should avoid. Of course, when I looked at James with my you're-being-a-judgmental-douchebag face, he immediately backtracked and said, "Well, you know, churches are like families. All of them have a few nuts. Those people could just be the exception to the rule there."

Yes, he was being judgmental, but he was right. I hate to admit it, but I should have listened to him.

*

Remember that disturbing trend we started of converting musicians to fill vacancies? Well, an incredibly talented singer (we'll call him Cole) started working side by side with James at his factory job. They had plenty of time to talk (somehow) about music that (conveniently) led to discussions of salvation versus damnation. At first, Cole wasn't having anything to do with the Jesus business. He was cocky and argumentative. His shit didn't stink. That religious stuff was fine but it wasn't for him. In essence, he was the living stereotype of a rock n' roll frontman.

But, as I've mentioned, once James had his mind made up he was like a pitbull clamped onto a mailman's juicy thigh. He even rounded our entire band up to go watch Cole's classic rock band (featuring Bill, our former guitarist and Mark, our first drummer) practice so we could scout his singing talent. At the time I don't remember having a problem with this, but, in retrospect, our arrogance had reached a whole new level. Here we were going to this heathen band's rehearsal with every intention of converting and stealing their lead singer. Again, we convinced ourselves that our main priority was really to deprive Satan of another victim. If he just so happened to join our band and make us rock stars then, well, that was just a fringe benefit, wasn't it?

Cole's beer swilling, profanity-spewing band sounded great (aside from their horrible bass player) and his singing practically had us drooling small ponds of saliva. They hammed it up (bands *always* have to show off when other musicians are watching) and ripped through a set of popular cock rock tunes of the day, but the one that stuck in my mind was "Eighteen and Life" by Skid Row. There aren't many vocalists with the pipes for that song but Cole didn't just do it justice, he ripped it a new asshole. And the members of Critical Dispatch were synchronized-spurting in their tighty whities.

We absolutely HAD to have this guy in our band!

I mean, the Lord absolutely HAD to save Cole's hellbound soul!

Of course, James eventually succeeded in converting Cole. We brought him over to audition and immediately everyone in the room knew that, together, this band was an undeniable force. Our songs sounded great but anything less than a stellar singer would doom us to the growing ranks of embarrassingly average (at best) Christian metal bands in the world. Now we not only had killer, twin-guitar riffs and a badass drummer but we also had the best rock singer in the area. Oh, and the bassist and keyboardist weren't bad either. It was time to hit some big time stages and begin our quest for world domination.

Chapter 21

My first visit to the Prophet's Guild revealed that the church was a rented, former department store in downtown Willard, OH. Its sanctuary had chairs arranged in a semi-circle around the barely-elevated pulpit's stage. Of course, the requisite potpourri was wafting through the air, just like VCF, but the praise and worship band paled in comparison. There was a little old lady playing piano and an effeminate guy with a salt n' pepper seventies mustache/permed mullet combo playing acoustic guitar. A guy with an un-curly ginger mullet joined in on bass guitar while Pastor Hilda banged away on a tambourine.

The preaching was purely emotional, as opposed to Pastor Scott's cerebral style, so that was a letdown. Jose and Hilda alternated on sermon duty but they didn't really have unique approaches. Every sermon started with the Holy Ghost speaking a special message to an attendee through either preacher. At first this seemed amazing to us, but we quickly caught on that this *miraculous* word from above was a gimmick aimed at first-time visitors, apparently in an attempt to hook them and reel them in. Then one of the Arroyos would begin with an Old Testament verse from one of the prophets and follow up with a bunch of vague prophecies about things like revival and blessings that would be coming our way if we (SHOCKER) handed over our hard-earned pay and stopped being such dirty, sinful pusbuckets. Once the congregation was worked up into a charismatic frenzy, the flailing about and speaking in tongues would begin. This usually led to altar calls for first time savings and rededications from wayward backsliders. Hands would be laid upon heads and bodies would hit the floor like twitchy bowling pins.

Even though the Prophet's Guild was less cerebral and more emotional, one thing that kept me coming back was the announcement that Jose and Hilda were starting a Bible college that would ordain ministers. Since I craved the intense, scholarly teaching that Pastor Scott always provided, my interest was piqued. I made it known that I wanted to be one of the first students signed up for this. The Arroyos beamed with pride, commended me for my "heart for the Lord", and assured me that they'd keep me posted.

Of course, while Missy had dropped out of college, I was still taking classes at our local Ohio State branch. My interest in these courses, though, had been flagging for quite some time, and my grades showed it. I was in love with the woman of my dreams. My band was getting bigger and bigger. The grocery store where I was employed offered to make me a management trainee. Why in the world would I want to keep paying thousands of dollars for an education that no longer interested me? All I needed was a legitimate excuse to keep my parents from going nuclear over my decision to drop out, and now I had it.

When that bomb dropped, I made sure to REALLY emphasize that I would soon reenter school through the Prophet's Guild. "No-no-no-no, Mom and Dad! This is just temporary! I decided to become a preacher instead of a teacher, that's all. I'll still get an education!"

For some reason the 'rents weren't buying it, possibly because none of their questions about the validity of a diploma from my cult's upcoming school could be answered. All I had to go on were some flimsy, pie-in-the-sky promises from two preachers who, in retrospect, may or may not have been officially ordained themselves. Since my bullheadedness was legendary and I was getting married soon anyway, Mom and Dad just gave up, stayed pissed, and stopped talking to me for several weeks. If their idiot son wanted to ruin his future by getting a fake diploma from a joke school then they weren't going to dignify his lunacy with any support whatsoever.

As it turns out, Mom and Dad had nothing to worry about. Okay, well, at the time they sure as shit did, but eventually all talk of a Bible college branching off from the church faded away. Our faithful pastors mentioned it less and less. Being the young-dumb-and-full-of-cum-moron that I was, the college's speed of erosion disappearance from the Prophet's Guild agenda didn't even register with me. You'd think that, if God had ordered the Arroyos to start such a learning institution, seeing it through would have been mandatory. I mean, scripture says that God isn't a man and He doesn't change, right? Well, when He's made in His worshippers' image He does. Fortunately for madcap preachers, their parishioners are usually so bogged down with the realities of day-to-day survival that minor broken promises and theological discrepancies often go undetected.

*

As for Critical Dispatch, our world domination began with an advertisement in the *Willard Times*. A new charity organization called Kids for Kids was hosting a talent show as a fundraiser. There was a cash prize ($100) for first place so clearly this was God providing an opportunity to fund our first E.P. of white-hot new tunes.

First, we had to meet with the massive, two-person staff of Kids for Kids to make sure their organization was on the up and up. Expecting two well-groomed, upper middle class folks, we instead met a lanky ex-hippy guy and his toothless, polyester-encased female compatriot. Both of them assured us that they believed in God and felt it was their mission to serve children in the community. It was obvious that they were the kind of folks who profess to be Christians but never set foot in church or cracked a Bible. Their hearts were in the right place, however it didn't take a rocket scientist to know that neither of them had a clue about launching a non-profit venture aiding disadvantaged youth. Honestly, they could have said and done anything short of drinking goat's blood from a pentagram-emblazoned skull and we'd still have been on board. Our eyes were full of stars and our hearts were set on recording a masterpiece that would secure a recording contract and world tour. So we paid our registration fee and skedaddled off to rehearse.

For some reason James was paranoid that the song we'd chosen to perform ("Sin's in Demand") didn't have enough explicitly Christian lyrics. We just couldn't take the chance that the massive crowd we'd most certainly be wowing might misconstrue our motives. I mean, what if they thought we were just in this for the money and fame? What if they knew that we were only really focused on evangelism when we needed a new band member? And what could we possibly do to make it ABSOLUTELY clear that we were all about being metal missionaries for Jesus?

"Oh, I know!" James exclaimed, racing upstairs to the practice room to turn on his keyboards.

We scampered after our beloved guru to see what seed the Holy Ghost was planting in his fertile mind now. Upon readying our respective instruments, James hit a key that produced an aircraft carrier's froggy alarm signal: AH-Ah-ah-ah-ah…

Pointing at Cole, James twitched with excitement, yelping, "That alarm will get everyone's attention, then we can all shout, 'We are soldiers of Jesus Christ!' to start the song! Then EVERYBODY will know what we stand for!"

Everyone grinned and immediately agreed that this was the most amazing idea in the history rock music, if not civilization itself. So James counted us off, sounded the alarm, we gang-vocaled our militant mania for the Messiah, and Darren ripped into the opening riff.

Instant songwriting gold!

HOLY SHIELD!

Our epic, Grammy-worthy momentum carried us through a bazillion rehearsals of "Sin's In Demand". Once we had that dead horse properly beaten, James, apparently full of Christian rock star humility, exclaimed, "Guys! We need to have a second song ready, just in case the crowd asks for an encore!"

"Yeah!" we all exclaimed unpretentiously.

"What song should we do?" I asked, imagining a rabid crowd demanding more tunes while we stood quavering and clueless onstage.

James' brow furrowed for a second, then his beady eyes lit up like a Christmas tree. "'One Hour for Life!'"

"Perfect!" Cole rejoiced. "Nobody will be confused about what we stand for with THAT song!"

Nothing says, "We're *so* happy you asked for another song!" like a tune about the perils of teen pregnancy and abortion, kids!

Chapter 22

As the Kids for Kids concert grew closer, the Prophet's Guild's services became stranger and stranger. Our preachers' habitual prophesying over new members and weird demands upon their congregation, although initially undetected, soon became obvious. On one occasion Hilda said that God, speaking through her, was ordering us to grab the Guild's flag and march around the sanctuary as His holy army. I remember hanging back at my seat, feeling awkward as hell, but peer pressure eventually pulled me into that Cuckoo Congo Line. To a certain extent, every service in that building felt odd, singing and carrying on with cars and pedestrians gawking at us through the huge picture window that was once used to display retail products, but this marching made us look even more like lemmings mindlessly migrating to a watery grave.

Nuttiness at this level almost made me ditch the Prophet's Guild. The logical side of my brain was screaming, *What the fuck are you doing? This is cult behavior!* But the emotional side that felt all warm and accepted there was smothering those thoughts with fluffy, white Holy Ghost pillows while murmuring, *Shhhh. Shhhh. Go to sleep, pesky brain. That's just the Devil trying to get you to question the ways of the Lord. Remember, His ways are above our ways and they confound the wise.*

*

Sometime after this, Missy found a job at a nursing home in Willard and needed a place to live in a hurry. She had no money for an apartment but didn't know anyone she could move in with. Of course, there was no way two self-respecting Christians would shack up like godless fornicators, especially when one of them is playing bass in a Bible-thumping metal band. Besides, abstaining from premarital sex was difficult enough when we *didn't* live under the same roof.

Go ahead and giggle and smirk skeptically about that last statement. No one in my family believed that we weren't banging like bunnies, either. Temptation certainly led us into about every activity except crossing home plate, but we were determined not to (totally) let the big J.C. down. In the short or long run I don't think it harmed our relationship. People are correct to say there's nothing to look forward to on your honeymoon (especially if you're dirt poor and can't afford a fancy trip to the Bahamas or Cancun) if you've already crossed that line. And sex definitely changes the dynamics of a relationship. The decision to abstain was one of the few from this time period, in regards to religion, that I wouldn't change. Do I pass judgment today on people who live together and bump uglies before marriage? Nope. But for us, at least, it was the right thing to do.

Jose and Hilda offered to let Missy use a bedroom in their glorious doublewide trailer, rent free, as long as she tithed and attended church whenever her work schedule allowed. While it wasn't the greatest experience for her, my beautiful bride to be did learn to cook some mighty tasty Mexican dishes. And, even though our relationship with them would eventually sour, the Arroyos' kind gesture was definitely appreciated.

Chapter 23

Now that we had our Kids for Kids setlist hammered out, it was time to focus on the most important element of our talent show gig: our costumes!

I remember (initially) disagreeing with James' disgust for bands who wore their street clothes onstage ("How can you tell who's in the band and who's just some Joe Blow in the crowd if everyone looks alike?") but, in all honesty, it didn't take much of a sales pitch to get this pasty white dork on board with glamming up. Before leaping aboard the heavenly metal express, I was jamming out to the likes of Poison, Hanoi Rocks, and Motley Crue. At that time a gentle breeze blowing out of the east could've convinced me to strap on some spandex and a frilly pirate shirt.

Of course, several band meetings were pretty much consumed with determining our outfits. Should each guy have a unique look? Would we look like morons if we all dressed alike, like Stryper, who resembled a hive of noisy bumblebees? In the end, James convinced us all that it was important to have a unifying theme to our attire. Thankfully, one of our biggest influences at the time was Skid Row so none of us ran out to purchase mascara, eye shadow and check-out-my-junk-in-braille spandex pants. Instead, we opted for denim jackets and ripped up jeans. Nobody had the chutzpah to wear the chain connecting an earring to a nose piercing, though.

Pansies!

*

On the day of the talent show, we were nervous but confident. Before loading up our gear to haul downtown, we circled up in our practice area for a pre-show prayer. At times like these, group prayers were often fraught with anxiety but this one was more of a "We know we're gonna nail this, God, but, just in case we need a little extra oomph, could you just kind of keep an eye out for us?" kind of thing.

When we arrived at the semi-trailer/band shell in the center of town, the Kids for Kids duo were apologetic because our competition only consisted of TWO other acts (one was a very good female singer but the other performer escapes my memory). They nervously assured us that the lack of contestants would not affect the promised amount of prize money (which it should have) and we reminded them that, even though this cash was crucial for financing the demo that would certainly lead to certain stardom, filthy lucre was NOT our motivation.

Another factor that worked in our favor was our placement on the bill: last. The first act to perform in a talent show pretty much NEVER wins. Why? People have short attention spans and they typically remember the performers from the middle of the bill to the end.

And so, it came to pass on this crisp, fall day that after the first two acts finished, Critical Dispatch took the stage, long hair stacked to the heavens with industrial strength hairspray (except for James who only had a budding fro and stach), fired up our amps, shouted, "WE ARE SOLDIERS OF JESUS CHRIST!" and tore Willard, OH a brand new, sanctified rectal orifice.

Not to boast, but I'm pretty sure at least thirty people (out of a crowd of around fifty) had to see their chiropractors for whiplash afterwards. It's been over two decades since that gimmicky entrance and I can still see that small audience's brains almost imploding from their ocular data violently clashing with the words echoing in their earholes.

WHAT?!

Young freaks with guitars are screaming about Jesus?!

WHAT?!

By the end of "Sin's in Demand" the terror we'd instilled in that tiny, midwestern crowd had magically transformed into boisterous applause. To this day I'm still shocked by the unanimous reaction we received. Folks in Ohio's portion of the Bible Belt don't often modify views formed from first impressions. The fact that we not only didn't die mid-song but were cheered back onto the stage for an encore was damn near equivalent to Jesus reaching into an empty basket and hauling out fish to feed a starving crowd.

After our anthemic, anti-abortion encore we huddled backstage for the requisite backslapping and congratulating while the judges tallied their scores. I only remember having one VERY brief pang of doubt about our chances of taking home the loot. *Seriously, that lady singer was pretty good. She's definitely more mainstream than we are! But, dude, did SHE get cheered back onto the stage for a second song? I think not!*

Of course, after what felt like several decades of anxious worrying, we were dragged back onstage and hailed as victors. Even though we were only being judged the best of three acts it still felt amazing. Never before in my nineteen years of existence had I competed and won at anything. I'm pretty sure the other guys in the band felt the same. So when the Kids for Kids folks asked us for a second encore, how could we say no?

*

After our triumphant encore, we strutted around the rest of the festival with our wives and girlfriends, chatting excitedly and basking in the glory of victory. But those joyful emotions didn't last long for all of us. Out of nowhere, Missy tugged my arm, pulling me aside to talk.

"What?" I asked, baffled by the angry look on her face.

"Shhh!" she hissed. "Keep your voice down."

Clueless as usual, I again inquired, "What's wrong?"

"Did you hear what James said to me?"

"When? I didn't even see you talking to him."

She scowled. "When you guys were playing I told Tom's girlfriend that I was hungry and she, apparently, thought I said that I was horny. She ran and tattled to James and he jumped my case about it!"

"What?! She told him that you said that?" Suddenly my post-gig buzz was dying a very speedy death.

"Yes!" Missy, clearly on the verge of tears, exclaimed.

"Well, it was just a misunderstanding. Don't worry about it."

My fiancé's angst escalated. "Aren't you going to say something to James?"

"Nah, it'll blow over," I reassured her. Of course, she was right. I should've nipped this brand new trend of snarky tattling and backstabbing in the bud but, at the time, I had no idea how much of a problem it would become.

Sadly, this trend was only half of the problem. The other (more important) half was my growing tendency to put the band before Missy. Throughout the course of Critical Dispatch's development, there were many, many attacks on my lady from the other wives, girlfriends, and band members. James was the biggest offender in this nonsense since he considered himself the Big Brother of the band but, did I defend Missy? I wish I could say that I did, but my responses were always lame remarks like, "Ah, that's just James. I wouldn't let it bother you. That's just the way he is."

It's a miracle that Missy stayed around.

Chapter 24

Somehow Critical Dispatch befriended a guy named Greg who'd just graduated from a recording school. A very reputable studio in Cleveland, OH had hired Greg but his boss wanted him to find some guinea pigs to record as an internship project. Of course, these musicians would still have to pay for studio time and tape. Oh yes, I said tape. There were no computers with ProTools in those days, kiddos.

Since we only had a measly $100 in our budget Greg convinced his boss to allow us to record for nothing but the price of the tape. What was the catch? We had to record on weekends between the hours of eleven p.m. and seven a.m. Six artsy types had to get creative and pull several all-nighters?

Oh, the horror!

We were in like sin, baby!

Of course the first round of sessions just had to be scheduled on the weekend of my big brother's wedding, which was also in Cleveland but there was no way I could fulfill my best man's duties after being up all night laying down bass and backing vocal tracks. It about ripped me in two, but I had to let the rest of the band go off to lose their recording studio cherries while I suffered through wedding festivities.

When I came home I couldn't wait to find out how amazingly glamorous the process of cutting tracks was, so I called Tom. "Dude!" I yelped into the phone. "What was it like? Was it awesome?"

Tom, sounding like I'd disturbed his dreams of Tama drums and Paiste cymbals, mumbled, "Yeah man, it was pretty intense. But there's a lot of sitting around while other guys are tracking. That gets boring real quick. Plus Greg took, like, four hours to get a drum sound for me...and he still goofed up one song so I'll have to redo it. And freakin' Gill kept redoing his solos over and OVER."

Admittedly, this didn't sound as fantastic I'd imagined but Tom was clearly just being a typically moody, prima donna drummer. "Well, Gill's a perfectionist. We want his solos to be rockin', right?"

"Yeah," Tom sighed. "But at a certain point it's like, dude, that's freakin' good ENOUGH. Let it go!"

"So what else happened?" I pried, anxious for something that cast my future recording experience in a more positive light.

"Man, I've been up for over twenty four hours. Can I just talk to you at practice in a couple days?"

Deflated, I grumbled, "Yeah, I guess. Later, man."

*

Other than being more anxious than a Satan-worshipping, crackhead, homosexual whore on Judgment Day, when I finally made it to the studio I laid my bass tracks down effortlessly and efficiently. Okay, the first song I added a track to sounds like shit all the way around (except for the vocals and keyboards) so most people don't notice how horribly stiff and safe I played. It was pretty intimidating to be recording in Sleeping Giant Studios (where the Cleveland Orchestra does its thing) so the fact that I loosened up and played well on the rest of the tunes is impressive.

The rest of this second weekend of recording was a monotonous blur of waiting around for the rest of the band to finish up. The most fascinating occurrence during this time was Tom having to re-record his high-hat cymbal because it sounded like crap in one song. He ended up performing the song with one real piece of drum gear, his high-hat, and the rest was all duct-taped studio padding. If you've never played drums then you probably can't appreciate how hard this was, but it's pretty much the equivalent of driving in a monsoon with your wiper blades on the lowest intermittent setting. If I remember correctly, he nailed it in one or two takes. Damn!

All in all it was an amazing experience that I wouldn't trade for anything. How many people can say they recorded in the basement of the NBC building in Cleveland? Not many, I'd wager. Of course, we'd find out later that the final product left a lot to be desired, but that's a tale for another chapter.

Chapter 25

Once my brother's (Catholic) nuptials and C.D.'s E.P. were out of the way, Missy and I began our pre-marital counseling at the Prophet's Guild. This was required if they were to marry us, which we'd requested, so I met with Jose and Missy met with Hilda once a week for a month or so. Being all atwitter about the whirlwind of wedding preparations, I don't remember anything that I was told in those sessions except for this one wacky tidbit of wisdom from Jose: "People will tell you to experiment with all kinds of things in the bedroom, but don't pay any attention to that. That's worldly talk. All you really need is the missionary position. That's good enough." Hell, during that time period I was just trying to keep from ripping my fiancé's clothes off and going to town. The thought of even worrying about experimenting with exotic positions wasn't even worth contemplating. Maybe his (or more likely: HILDA's) holy and monotonously dogmatic stance on this was what led to him cheating on Hilda with the church organist a few years after this. I'll never know.

And what was Pastor Hilda's womanly wisdom for Missy? Mainly she encouraged us to not wait to procreate. God would provide financially if we had faith because it was His will that we be fruitful and multiply. Oh, and Missy was also urged to quit her job because the Lord wanted her to stay home to cook and clean for her man. How modern and cutting edge, especially coming from a female pastor who clearly relished wearing the pants at home and in the sanctuary!

After we were married we felt TONS of pressure to comply with both of these admonitions and were treated as wayward lambs when no children were popping out of Missy's gainfully employed body. Never mind the fact that we could barely support our own young asses, let alone a brood of offspring's young asses! Thankfully we stuck to our guns and didn't cave to pastoral pressures.

*

Along with our awkward premarital counseling, Missy and I quickly found ourselves swirling in family drama. As soon as we declared that our service would be in a protestant church, word spread like an STD at a swinger's convention and many of my relatives were up in arms.

First my mom threw a fit: "Why can't you get married in the Catholic church like your brother?!"

Then my paternal grandmother (Granny) announced that she was boycotting our wedding.

Next, my maternal grandmother followed suit, declaring her impending absence from our joyous celebration.

Add all of that pressure on top of the stress we were already under about picking dresses, tuxedos, invitations, guests, a photographer, DJ, and bridesmaids and groomsmen (James and his wife refused to be involved because they were "done" spending money on being in wedding parties) and you have two very frazzled youngsters. My relatives were all applying direct (boycotting) or indirect (hinting that a Catholic service would keep the peace) pressure that nearly made our heads explode.

When Missy's dad heard, he made a very kind offer: elope and he'd give us all the money he'd spend on the wedding and reception to get started in life. We immediately said, "YES!" but, alas, Missy's mother stepped in to declare, "You are not going to take MY party away from me!"

The illusion that this was OUR celebration of OUR love for one another was quickly and very publically executed.

But we stuck to our guns on the protestant ceremony, for better or worse.

Oh, and all who threatened to boycott were in attendance. And they even behaved themselves!

*

Shortly before we were married, Missy found a tiny apartment that we would eventually share after our honeymoon. She had barely settled in when one of our fellow Prophet's Guild members asked to visit so he could deliver some early wedding presents. This guy, we'll call him Glenn, had thick, black square glasses, curly hair, a moustache, and the most effeminate mannerisms I'd witnessed at that time. In the past he'd confided in me about his "unnatural desires" that were caused by demons that had to be cast out by Jose and Hilda. Supposedly, thanks to this dequeerification exorcism, he was now healed of the homo sickness and waiting patiently for God to deliver his *female* soulmate.

On the night of Glen's visit, Missy and I sat on our tiny love seat and awkwardly waited while our friend struggled up the second story apartment's stairs with our gifts. Just about any interaction with Glenn made us feel at least a little nervous but we were pleasantly relieved when he lugged first one then two end tables into our tiny living room. They were used and a little ratty, but we were grateful for any furniture. After we thanked him and chatted for a while, Glenn said he had one more present for us that he'd have to fetch from his car. Our guard was down at this point so we probably just assumed he had a lamp to plop on one of the end tables.

Not quite!

Instead, we received an illuminating gift of another sort: a how-to book on sex that explained the ins and outs of intercourse. This glorious tome was stuffed with scientific diagrams, advice from counselors, and pictures of steamy carnal action. And this book did *not* agree with Pastor Jose's stance on the One True Sexual Position!

SCORE!

Glenn, nervously noting that our jaws had dropped to our knees, quickly explained that "Sex isn't everything in a relationship, but it's important and I want you two to be happy and fulfilled in the bedroom. There's nothing sinful about a husband and wife consummating their holy commitment. This book explains just about everything you need to know." His speech managed to ease the weirdness somewhat, but Glenn didn't stick around long after he was through with it. Awkwardness came naturally to him but so did intelligence. Clearly he realized that we needed some time to process this special gift. At the time I couldn't grasp his motivation but today I'm convinced he was attempting to live vicariously through us. If he couldn't engage in a healthy, committed, sexual relationship, then he could at least help two friends do so.

Back then I was quite sheltered and had never been around any gay folks but it's painfully obvious now that this poor guy's religious brainwashing was keeping him bound, gagged, and tortured in the closet. At one point, after we were married, he discreetly asked us to subscribe to his favorite clothing catalog (the name of which escapes me) because he still lived with his parents and they had forbidden it in their home. I may have been incredibly naïve at the time, but when that first catalog arrived and I flipped through it, even I could see that something was a tad odd about it. All of the clothing was for men, so obviously all of the models were dudes—but they were all impeccably tan, well groomed, and muscular. Maybe I was just a small town hick but none of my guy friends wore mesh pirate shirts to display their six-pack abs or G-strings that accentuated their glorious ASSets.

Poor Glenn! I haven't heard from him in many, many years but I hope he's been able to shake off those God shackles and live as a free man. With any luck he's flaunting his fabulousness somewhere with HIS partner of choice. No one should be condemned to self-torture over something they had no control over. I know I didn't wake up one day and decide to be attracted to curvy ladies' boobs and booties. Besides, I'm pretty sure Jesus NEVER mentioned homosexuality but He sure did stress the importance of not casting stones.

Oh, and LOVE and ACCEPTANCE seemed pretty high in his estimation as well.

*

184

Our wedding ceremony, unlike the following description of it, was painfully long and drawn out. Missy and I were both intensely nervous, stressed, and exhausted from all of the drama of planning our (more accurately: my mother-in-law's) special day so we were hoping the shindig would be brief and pleasant.

WRONG!

Not that we were completely ignorant of what a Prophet's Guild wedding entailed; we'd had rehearsal, but our husband and wife preacher team failed to mention that their tag-team sermonizing would drag on ad nauseam until all in attendance prayed for death. Just when all of us thought every Bible verse concerning matrimony had been shared, one of the Arroyos would babble on for another millennium about this most sacred covenant and what it meant. And then the other would remember a zillion other verses to machinegun at us. Nobody in our families complained at the time, but I distinctly recall that my mother only watched the VHS tape of the festivities once, whereas the recording of my big brother's wedding had practically been worn out over the years. Of course his wedding was the ultimate Catholic extravaganza so that may have had *something* to do with that.

Love ya, Mom!

Chapter 26

Critical Dispatch's first big concert celebrating the release of our E.P. (titled: *Fate of the Wicked*) was booked at Willard High School. Tom, still working as a pizza delivery guy, came up with a genius marketing plan: convincing his manager to allow us to glue ads for our show on their boxes. Willard isn't that huge (population 6,000) so there aren't that many pizza joints. Our ad being delivered (for free!) to hundreds of homes for two weeks straight was a massive coup.

We even had concert shirts silkscreened for the occasion. They had our logo on the front and the title of our newest, catchiest tune ("Make It Right") emblazoned on the back. When we proudly showed them to Glenn, he gave us shit about the shirts because they "didn't make our Christian message clear enough". This accusation was constantly being leveled at us so we took it with a grain of salt.

Oh, and this gig was scheduled a mere week after my wedding. I was so brainwashed and psychotically devoted to this band that I convinced my wife to cut our honeymoon short so we could return in time for pre-concert rehearsals. Of course, we were so dirt poor that our elaborate honeymoon consisted of a three day stay at the Quaker Square Hilton in Akron, OH, but STILL! In an ideal world a man will only get married once and I limited my one and only honeymoon to a few days. Talk about putting my band ahead of my bride! And this certainly wasn't the one and only time I did such a thing. Trust me!

Having an E.P. to sell elevated our professional status considerably, but our look needed an overhaul in order complete the picture. Too many bands, we decided, had great albums but half-assed their live presentation. Critical Dispatch would NOT be guilty of this. So Gill wore a glam ensemble that included a blazer, neon pink pants, and cowboy boots. Cole wore a woman's black and metallic gold blouse, black pants, and boots. James and Tom wore outfits that were similar to the others'. I wore a homemade black tank top with crosses bleached into it and ripped up jeans (decorated with the band's logo all over the legs) with black and blue spandex pants beneath them. And Darren? Well, he showed up in a black t-shirt, jeans, and grass-stained tennis shoes, which nearly sent James into hysterics.

On the night of the big show, I remember being completely terrified. Here we were, about to perform in the auditorium of the high school in which I was constantly reminded that I was a nonentity with no future. What if nobody showed up? What if a bunch of people did come and we made fools of ourselves?

It turned out that I had nothing to fear. Tom's ingenious marketing plan was a roaring success. There were at least 150 attendees, many of whom were quite vocally appreciative of our performance. Sure, there were the typical live show snags (broken guitar strings, etc.) but our big hometown debut was quite successful. I have no idea how *Fate of the Wicked* sold that night but I do know that our t-shirts did well because I recall seeing people wearing them that night and later around town. Now that I think about it, I also remember hearing cars driving by our rehearsal space with our E.P. booming from their stereo systems and Tom growling, "I KNOW that guy never bought our tape! People are burning copies instead of buying them!"

Yeah, computer-obsessed teenagers didn't invent music piracy. It was going on way before that.

Embarrassingly enough, some of the screaming, t-shirt-wearing kids from that night found out where several of us lived and began leaving gifts and stalking us. James found a present with a lovely note on his porch. My wife and I (both working third shift at the time) were awakened by teens screaming "Critical Dispatch!" outside our apartment. It was both flattering and scary.

Of course it was quite easy for me to take all of this adulation and success in stride, being a misfit with horrible self-esteem, right?

Right.

Chapter 27

After the hitching and honeymooning had finally occurred, Missy and I settled into a steady routine of attending three weekly services at the Prophet's Guild. Oh yeah, we were one of those Wednesday night, Sunday morning, and Sunday evening kind of couples who even helped out with Children's Church (the cry room for you Catholics). We were sold out to Jesus and didn't care who knew it.

Hallelujah!

Praise His holy name!

Around this time, the biggest trend in Christianity was the concept of spiritual warfare. Frank Peretti's bestselling books, *This Present Darkness* and *Piercing the Darkness*, popularized this fixation on the powers of good and evil clashing in a realm unseen to human eyes. I remember reading these thick, intense, page-turners and being completely fascinated with the concept of humanity's words and actions affecting the angelic and demonic forces around us. Soon after the books exploded in popularity, preachers all over the globe were latching onto this concept of spiritual warfare, using it to excite stagnant congregations' passion for prayer and warn them about the dangers of careless actions.

Jose and Hilda took to this sermon-fodder like cats to tuna steaks. They began to constantly harp on the negative effects of stray thoughts and ill-chosen words. Then they'd rail on believers who allowed the Devil into their homes via rock n' roll, movies, pagan statues, and satanic children's games. Their sermons included wild tales of believers who were troubled by demonic manifestations (God would temporarily give them insight into the spirit realm and they'd see demons flitting about in their homestead, etc.) until they woke up, kicked the Devil out (with prayer) and rededicated the house to Jesus.

Of course my brain, which specializes in being overly active and creative when I try to fall asleep, became obsessed with the spiritual warfare sermons. One night, as Missy and I were lying in bed just after turning the lights out, things came to a head. Our tiny apartment's bedroom walls were mostly adorned with various clown-themed items, remnants of my new bride's teenage bedroom, such as Mardi Gras masks and circus clowns. Other than being afraid that a friend would see these feminine decorations and demand that I hand over my Man Card, these objects had never bothered me but, at that moment, a massive wave of paranoia swept over me. I became convinced that those infernal, evil clowns were causing some recent financial and familial negativity in our lives. Many theorize that clowns represent death, so that made them footholds for the Devil to infiltrate our sanctuary and besiege us with his demonic soldiers.

At first I tried to ignore these thoughts and doze off but it was impossible. After tossing and turning for a while I confided in Missy about my fears. Usually talking things out with a trusted confidant helps me see how unjustified my anxiety is, but on that night my paranoia, instead of being alleviated, became contagious. You see, our brains were Perettified and marinating in spiritual warfare indoctrination so she too was able to instantly find other examples of recent hardship that had to have come from those damnable clowns.

As we traded stories of Satan's recent attacks on our lives we succeeded in escalating ourselves into an even more heightened state of panic. Suddenly, headlights from cars on the street seemed to cast sinister shadows that slithered to and fro on our walls like demons circling and ready to pounce. Normal, everyday sounds in our apartment and neighborhood seemed to emanate from the depths of Hell. Then, an eerie, suffocating quiet settled over the building and sat on our chests, forcing our hearts to beat harder and our lungs to strain for breath. It felt like the calm before a mighty storm and the tiniest sound probably would have shocked us into full-blown fight or flight mode.

"What should we do?" Missy whispered.

I gulped and whispered back, "Let's pray about it."

So we joined our cold, clammy hands in the dark and begged for guidance. After ten or fifteen minutes of desperate intercession, the answer became clear: the clowns. We absolutely MUST get rid of those insidiously creepy clowns. God was revealing to us that these decorations were beacons for Lucifer's Legions. It was time to purge our home and rededicate it to Jesus!

We scrambled out of bed, grabbed a trash bag, and de-clowned the entire apartment. Every single last one of those ghoulish bastards grinned all the way down into Hefty Bag Hell. Then we turned on our porch light and tiptoed out to the apartment building's trashcans. Missy lifted the lid and I crammed the jettisoned jesters in and clamped the lid down over them as we heaved heavy sighs of relief. Once we returned to our apartment, in imitation of our charismatic preachers' dramatic tales, we went from room to room, praying and rededicating our home to Jesus. Then, finally, we were able to crawl back into bed and sleep.

Of course, after that, we never had a single ounce of misfortune in our lives. Each day was full of cotton candy, sunshine, and rainbows. Satan was reduced to pouting miserably on his throne of skulls. His minions had failed to defeat our guardian angels in combat and his plans for our lives were forever thwarted. Oh if only all believers had the cajones to ditch their clowns!

Actually, this spiritual warfare doctrine only lead to an even more maddening state of solipsism, for me at least. Since I'd learned that my every physical and mental deed sent ever-widening ripples out into the spirit realm, impacting my existence and the happiness of those around me, life became torture, especially at work.

You see, as a third shift grocery store wage slave, there was usually too much time alone stocking shelves in a (mostly) dark supermarket. In between being freaked out by nearly every sound or jumping in fear of my own shadow, I remember analyzing, reanalyzing, then re-reanalyzing my behavior, constantly begging God for forgiveness: *Lord Jesus, I know I don't deserve your mercy, but please forgive me for getting testy with my coworker. And I shouldn't have been singing along with that secular rock song in front of the stock crew last night. That is NOT a good witness for them to see me enjoying the world's music instead of yours. And I'm SO sorry that I noticed how attractive that new cashier is. I'm a happily married man and I know your Word says that I've already committed adultery by looking at her lustfully, but I hope you wash me clean with your precious blood.*

As I wrung every last ounce of joy from my own life, I was completely oblivious to the insanity of this spiritual warfare doctrine. How in the FUCK can anyone stay psychologically healthy while being so painfully self-aware? And isn't being convinced that your every thought, word, or deed could have earth-shattering repercussions the very epitome of narcissism? How much more egocentric could someone *possibly* be?

But, then again, isn't most Christian dogma self-absorbed? God created life, but only on *our* planet. God watches our every move, judging us for eternity. He created all animals to serve us. Humans aren't another species of animals; we're the apex of His creative endeavors. If someone accepts Jesus as his personal savior, then it's possible to have a personal relationship with the Creator of the Universe. God will speak to you and guide you, in between watching over the orbits of planets, wars between countries, keeping the Pope safe from assassins, and intervening in sporting events.

Sure, there are many exhortations to selfless behavior in the Bible but, as the cliché goes, the proof's in the pudding. Many Christian organizations feed the hungry, clothe the naked, and visit those in prison, but there are always strings attached. "We'll give you food IF you let us preach at you. Here are some free clothes, brother. Have you heard the Good News of Jesus Christ? How are the prison guards treating you? No, the Lord doesn't think your crimes are beyond His mercy. The Blood of Christ can wash away any sin. Yes, you're saved by faith alone, but if you don't walk the walk then you'll be the tasty human marshmallow in a Satanic S'more in HELL!"

If the belief in Christ is such an ennobling transformation, why do the most religious areas in the U.S.A. (and other countries, for that matter) have the most hate toward those who are different? Racism walks hand in hand with intense religious belief; the KKK, after all, proudly proclaims that it is a Christian organization, not a hate group. Joseph Smith, the founder of Mormonism, believed that the color of a black person's skin came from God's curse upon Ham, Noah's son. Religion fosters other social injustices such as homophobia and misogyny. Christianity's control over the United States' conservative party has led to women being denied control over their own bodies. Islam teaches that women are second class citizens who must cover their bodies and submit to men at all times. According to a study (Cross-National Correlations of Quantifiable Societal Health with Popular Religiosity and Secularism in the Prosperous Democracies) conducted by the Kripke Center, "There is evidence that...the strongly theistic, anti-evolution south and mid-west [have] markedly worse homicide, mortality, STD, youth pregnancy, marital and related problems than the northeast where societal conditions, secularization, and acceptance of evolution approach European norms." And there are, obviously, other studies that confirm these findings.

So where is the redemptive power of religious belief to be found then?

The proof, as the old saying goes, is in the pudding.

195

Maybe I'm wrong but all of this madness seems to trace back to the inherent self-absorption of religion. If the whole universe revolves around me, I'm created in God's image, and women are a sparerib byproduct of men, then how tolerant am I going to be of a Muslim, homosexual, or woman? Jesus (and George W. Bush) said that we're either with Him or against Him, so them damn Mohammed worshippin' camel jockeys are the enemy. Leviticus orders us to kill gays so it has to be those poop pirates and muffin munchers who're are bringing God's wrath down on 'Merica! Plus, if the Bible has all the answers worth knowin' and it warns me not to get too high fallutin' full of myself and what my tiny, tiny brain pan can do, then imagination and education (unless they make me money for a big ole pick up truck and a bazillion guns) are for sissies and queers!

Is it just me or did that last paragraph become redder in the neck as it progressed?

Chapter 28

The pizza box advertising campaign was a huge success but not all of Critical Dispatch's marketing ideas were winners. We once spent a big chunk of cash for a graphic designer to whip up a full-page advertisement for *Fate of the Wicked*. This incredibly sharp ad featured our band photo appearing to burn its way through the paper, with the slogan: "Too Hot to Hide! Burning in the Message with an Innovative Commercial Edge!" Then we coughed up another huge ball of dough to place this masterpiece in Christian metal's number one magazine: *Heaven's Metal* (now simply called *HM Magazine*).

At best, this advertisement netted us two or three mail orders for the E.P.

YOUCH!

Apparently we WEREN'T too hot to hide.

*

Our marketing may have been hit or miss, but we got a lesson in how it's done when we were booked to play at a weeklong youth retreat at a church in Norwalk, OH. The youth pastor, Matt, had the brilliant idea of having us close out the last three days of the get-together. On Thursday night we played just one song, teasing the kids and showing them what they had to look forward to if they kept coming. Then we played three songs on Friday night, further whetting their appetites.

By Saturday night, after two days straight of being rock n' roll blue-balled, those kids were ready to explode, which they did as soon as we kicked into our full set. Along with screaming their brains out, they were launching themselves over our rented monitors and onto the stage. At one point we had to stop the set because they had broken one of the speakers. Cole pleaded with them to have a good time without annihilating the equipment. Of course, they calmed down a tiny bit for a couple songs, then immediately resumed their imitations of horny chimpanzees hopped up on meth. We half-heartedly pleaded for calmness then promptly just gave in to their enthusiasm and enjoyed it.

Throughout the whole week we'd been continuously impressed by Pastor Matt. He was so hip, intelligent, and charismatic that people couldn't help but love him. Everyone could tell that he was doing great things for the teens in his community.

A year or two later, though, we received word that Matt was fired by his church for having a sexual relationship with a teen girl from his congregation. Finding this out was incredibly crushing and disillusioning. We were totally suckered in by this guy's charm. None of our "pedophile" radars had even beeped in his presence. Were we that horrible at judging people? And how could God let that perv go around boinking young girls like that? Shouldn't He have protected her from all of the shame, trauma, and humiliation that this relationship would bring upon her?

Apparently not.

Is God's insistence on adult authority figures having free will more important than keeping a girl from being violated?

But I guess I shouldn't judge the Judge because I'm *completely certain* He was using her statutory rape for a higher cause that my puny brain cannot comprehend.

*

After our stint as the house band for a pedophile, we (somehow) managed to get booked at the Ohio State Fair, a Christian metal festival in Monroe, OH, and a massive Christian rock festival in Virginia (Finally! A paying gig!).

I would be remiss if I didn't mention the freeloading nature of most Christian concert promoters. A typical phone conversation with one of these cretins went something like this:

"Hi. My name's Billy Bob. Can y'all drive down to West Virginia to play at our church? We get lots of big bands down here and we can pack the place!"

"How much does your venue pay?" James would respond.

"Well, most bands are in this business *to save souls*, not money. But I *guess* we could pass a hat to maybe give y'all a little gas money. Plus you can sell your music and merchandise, right?"

At first we let these cheapskates guilt trip us into playing pro bono but after losing our asses several times we decided to demand respect by asking them to sign a contract guaranteeing that, at a minimum, our travel expenses would be met. Some promoters responded well and paid us but most passed on us after insinuating that we were greedy, worldly, and *very* un-Christlike. Of course, if a show offered big-time exposure then we were perfectly willing to pay-to-play. What band isn't?

*

Anyway, the Critical Dispatchmobile (as the dingy RV beast we were making payments on was dubbed) had bunk beds in the rear and a dining area with 1970s brown plaid cushioned benches that could double as beds for band members. We even had a tiny potty in which to piss because, if you don't know the rules of tour bus travel, there's no pooping because the grey water tank keeps the turds swimming and stinking just beneath you at all times. Of course, cram six male musicians in such a tiny

200

space and you can be assured that the aroma of ass and armpits will be the norm anyway, but still: everyone has limits.

So now we were set for travel and no reasonable gig opportunities would be turned down since transportation was no longer an issue. Nothing could hold us back from blazing trails all over our fine nation! World domination was mere millimeters away!

Since we needed a warm-up show for the big festival down south, we booked a gig in a tiny town about fifteen to twenty miles away. It was *so* exciting to be able to roll out like rock stars, crammed into our own transport with guitars, amps and drums. We couldn't wait for our adoring fans to gasp in awe as we strutted down the RV's steps like the glamorous gods of metal that we were. "Woah, dude! They have their own tour bus! They're too amazing for our shitty little town. They should have Bon Jovi opening for THEM!"

Giggling and high-fiving like grade school kids, we set out for the gig. Tom bounced up and down on his seat like an ADHD kid hopped up on crack, a shit-eating grin plastered on his face as he drummed his sticks on the table. The rest of us sprawled luxuriously in the other seats and bunk beds, gawking out the windows, pretending we were jaded rock stars on the way to yet another faceless town.

About halfway to the show a loud gunshot noise, followed by violent swerving, killed our fantasizing. Fortunately, James was driving and his expertise behind the wheel saved us from a gruesome tumble into a deep ditch beside a farmer's field. Instead we careened and wobbled to a halt in the gravel beside the road. All pretenses of being seasoned rock veterans had drained from our faces to be replaced by shaken, fearful rookie expressions.

"What happened?!" I yelped. "Did we hit something?"

We tumbled shakily out the door to gawk at our glorious transport. It must've been quite the sight for the assortment of rednecks driving by: six longhaired freaks poking their heads into all four wheel wells at once. Within seconds James, using his virtuoso mechanical intellect, diagnosed the problem: a flat tire. Apparently we didn't have the foresight to determine that six musicians, their instruments, and an entire PA system might pose a problem for an ancient, rickety rustbucket. Perhaps the Lord blew our tire to keep us dimwits from shining our limited light on His flock. Or, better yet, if we couldn't handle the glory of playing tiny hick towns, the gospel pavilion at the state fair, and two big festivals, without our egos ballooning, then how could He trust us with real tours and a recording contract? Surely He was protecting us from our own prideful flesh, right?

Or, more likely, we were just six dumbasses who failed to consider the laws of physics and thus had to cancel a gig that could've helped make a loan payment.

Another episode I was involved with while the spiritual warfare fad raged on was an educational boycott. Willard City Schools had a new elementary curriculum that focused on fantasy literature in an effort to foster students' imagination and instill a love of reading. Once the Prophet's Guild caught wind of this blasphemy, our pastors helped other local churches lead a charge to bully the school board into banning these insidious lessons that surely promoted witchcraft and Satanism. Jose and Hilda fired up the faithful with messages like: "The Devil is coming after our children and we MUST put a stop to it, brothers and sisters! We must rise up and pack that school board meeting and show them that we WILL intervene on behalf of our sons and daughters! Let the Church say, 'Satan, these are OUR children and you CANNOT have them!'"

Of course, I babbled their nonsense on this issue to whoever would listen, much to my embarrassment today. An elementary teacher lived next door to my parents and when she complained about the protests I demonstrated my supremely closed mind by going off on her in a self-important demonstration of righteous indignation and jackassery. All the poor woman could do was blink and gape as this Bible-thumping asswipe, who used to listen to Motley Crue and Guns n' Roses with her son, spewed hellfire and brimstone into her face.

Like my peers in churches throughout town, I never even thought to research this curriculum or think for myself. Obviously my pastors had done their homework. They'd never go off half-cocked in a crusade against the schools. Their word was as good as gold, right?

To quote Dr. Evil (from the Austin Powers movies): "How about NO, Scott!"

By the time the shit was done hitting the fan, Willard's school board folded like a homeless guy's cardboard house in a windstorm. The curriculum they'd spent thousands and thousands of dollars on was given the holy heave ho and it was back to basics time once again. Screw that whimsical witchcraft and sorcery nonsense! School was meant to be painfully boring. The Three Rs, much like the King James Bible, were good enough for St. Paul so they're good enough for our youngins!

This is an embarrassing chapter of my life that I've never mentioned until this book. Today, as a veteran teacher who's had religious parents after his hide, the mere act of typing these words makes me cringe and my palms sweat. Occasionally parents have called my bosses to complain about literature that I use and it pisses me off to no end. At work I maintain a (mostly) calm and professional demeanor about it but at home the rants go something like this: "Goddamn religious fanatics! There's nothing in that story worse than anything from Edgar Allen Poe! What the fuck is wrong with them? If they want their little angel protected from the real world why don't they send him to a damn Christian school?" And then it hits me like a pimp slap to the face: *Oh yeah, I was one of those douchebags once. They're just doing what they think is best. Their culture is so insular that they don't know any better. Sigh. I'll just provide an alternative story for the kid. No big deal.*

And then, to make myself feel better, I buy a little trinket from EvolveFish.com, listen to an episode of *The Thinking Atheist* podcast, and remind myself that, thankfully, some religious fanatics manage to break free from mental bondage.

Still, if I could hop aboard a time machine and erase my part in that little book-banning episode I probably would.

Chapter 29

Since the Critical Dispatchmobile's maiden voyage ended ingloriously, we decided to prevent further mishaps by renting U-Haul trailers for our gear. We still had to cram Tom's drums into the RV's tiny bathroom but the cramped quarters did absolutely nothing to dampen our spirits, especially when we had back-to-back shows at high profile events!

Our first gig was at the Ohio State Fair, but it was only memorable because:

1.) A psycho street preacher type dude was yelling at a lady in a red dress (because red is the color of SATAN!) and us (because the bass drum is the heartbeat of the DEVIL!).

2.) We played through a primo PA system that was manned by a world-class soundman who made us sound so good it didn't matter that there were only ten to twenty people watching. If you've never played live then you may not appreciate this, but this guy made our performance sound like a killer, polished professional's CD playing through the stage monitors. A small-time soundman kills musicians' eardrums with screaming feedback and a jumbled mess of instrumentation blaring from the monitors that makes it impossible to enjoy the gig.

Immediately after this show, we left for Hamilton, OH to play at the Rock Force Music Fest, held at the infamous Solid Rock Church (mostly known for their sixty-two foot high Touchdown Jesus statue that was struck by lightning and burned in 2010, while the Hustler Super Store across the highway was, incidentally, mercifully spared). On the way to this illustrious venue, our crappy RV began malfunctioning. We made it to Hamilton, barely, after stopping on the way so James and Gill could spend nearly the entire night struggling to fix the behemoth while the rest of us tried to catch some shuteye inside.

Needless to say, we were six exhausted, grumpy S.O.B.s when we arrived to load in at the Solid Rock compound. Aside from the aforementioned Jesus statue, the rest of the place resembled a massive dude ranch financed by Texas oil money. The buildings, connected by a tiny, paved road, were covered in a rustic, faux-stucco finish on the outside, but we were *totally* unprepared for their interiors.

We stumbled into the main sanctuary, bleary-eyed and cranky but expecting a familiar church vibe that would soothe our battered souls. Instead, as we shuffled through with our guitars, gaping openly at the Vegas-level perversion around us, we found a disgustingly gaudy mega-church with a massive neon dove hanging from the ceiling. After the C.D. equipment had been loaded in and we'd soundchecked, we sought out a place to change into our stage clothes. A Rock Force Music Fest staff member directed us to an assistant pastor's office. Even more gaping ensued as we encountered real marble furniture and walls plastered with pictures of said pastor (a former Christian body builder who apparently LOVED his own promo pics).

Narcissism and materialism are next to godliness, right?

All of this glitz and glam sent poor, frazzled James over the edge. He ranted and raved about what a sickening display of debauchery the place was. The rest of us joined in readily, bitching about the hypocrisy of it all as if we were all water-walking examples of Christlike righteousness. Right when our gripefest was reaching its crescendo, the door cracked open and a rocker with long, flowing blonde hair asked if he could come in to get dressed. Once again, we were gaping in awe, but not because of the Solid Rock's disgustingness. This dude was Bruce Swift, lead guitarist of the headlining band: Sacred Warrior!

Mr. Swift's band was a universal favorite in the C.D. camp so, when he lectured us about not casting the first stone, we were all completely mortified--except James, that is. James was clutching onto his self-righteous angst for dear life. Our fearless leader argued and argued, futilely laboring to sway Bruce to his point of view. Until, eventually, Mr. Swift agreed to disagree and calmly left James to fume on his own.

We still managed to play a killer set with very few hitches. I was feeling particularly outgoing so I really hammed it up onstage. At one point my antics must have been getting on Darren's nerves because, in between songs, he leaned over toward my ear and mockingly laughed, "Do you think you can hog the spotlight any more?" Maybe I could get a little needy for attention onstage from time to time, but I remember this irritated me into taming my behavior down for maybe a song before I thought to myself, *Screw him! All he does is stand there like a freakin' bookend. I'm having a blast, this crowd digs us, and I'm going to seize the day!*

All bands have members who fight for the spotlight and have jealousy-fueled feuds over perceived slights. We were all running on fumes and short-tempered at this point so I don't harbor any ill feelings over this, but I do think that our Christianity caused more nitpicking and backstabbing than it alleviated. We were all endlessly examining each other under microscopes, just waiting for something to bitch about. Sure, all of this is typical musician crap, but the added factor of the invisible savior in the room created an endless feedback loop of self-righteous witch hunt drama that, much like the Solid Rock pastor's self-infatuation, never ended.

Chapter 30

Missy and I continued to attend church three times a week, study the bible, and tithe our ten percent, which, of course, made our marriage glide along like butter across a hot skillet.

Well, not exactly.

Unfortunately, as our submersion in nondenominational doctrine deepened, so did my intolerance for all things secular. My sermon-pickled brain could only see reality in terms of black and white, which caused more and more marital friction. If Missy rented a movie that had disturbing elements in it then, as I'd been taught at church, it was my husbandly duty to insist that we avoid such entertainment. When I didn't see my wife studying scripture every night before bed, I expressed concern about her spirituality suffering from malnourishment. Oh, and God forbid I should catch Missy listening to a secular rock station on the radio! "Honey, we can't listen to that! It doesn't edify the Lord!"

To her credit, Missy almost always kept her cool with my idiocy. She made it clear that she disagreed with me and she wasn't going to buy into my legalistic (Christianese for: extremely purist) worldview, which frustrated me to no end. Why couldn't she see that even a little bit of tolerance for secular culture created a slip n' slide ride that ended in the infernal pits of Hell!?! Wasn't she listening to the same sermons I was? How could Missy say she loved the Lord while being so careless with her spiritual wellbeing?

And so, obviously, we argued more and more. At the time I was too stupid to see how controlling I was because the church, which was dominating my life, was constantly telling me that the man of the house had to run a tight ship. The husband was the captain and if anyone on board went down, it was his fault.

To this day I have no clue why Missy didn't divorce my sorry ass. What she needed was a supportive, loving partner, not a biblical babysitter who watched her every move. Hell, she already had plenty of people (people at church, Critical Dispatch bandmembers and their significant others, etc.) keeping her under a microscope; the last thing she needed was another one at home.

*

Fortunately for us, being rational people, this zealotry could only last so long and, oddly enough, we had our shitty jobs to thank. Working long hours, often on different shifts from each other, caused plenty of mental and physical exhaustion that helped overcome a lot of that external pressure. *Go to church on Sunday night? But I have to get some sleep before slaving away on the stock crew. Wednesday night services? But we haven't been home and conscious at the same time all week! I miss my wife!*

Still, any failure to attend was usually followed by a guilt trip that only two formerly Catholic preachers could be travel agents for. At first our absences merely caused Jose and Hilda to smile and politely ask if we'd been ill. The concern was *completely* parental and *for our own good.* Then the smiles became more strained, stretching across their condescending faces as they reminded us about God rewarding *faithful* servants. Then, content like this would be (coincidentally) woven into their sermons: "Satan is just waiting with baited breath for believers to stray from the path. His demons will fill God's people's heads full of doubts about scripture and their hearts will be full of prideful rebellion!"

Our shepherds were obviously growing more and more agitated. Eventually frowning, shaking heads that barely masked hostility replaced smiles. *How DARE these ungrateful little twits do this to us after all we've done for them!* Their homilies intensified: "Yahweh is a jealous God and He will NOT tolerate this. His protective shield will not encompass people who insist on being unfaithful!"

As you can imagine, over time the puppet strings they were pulling became visible and our resentment eroded any guilt over disappointing the two preachers who'd bent over backwards to help us when few others would. Yes, we appreciated their assistance, but Jose and Hilda had clearly become different people since then, as had we. Before we were wayward misfits with no support structure to speak of and they were gentle, loving parental adults who had patience with us. Now, Missy and I had each other and our confidence in our adult decision-making was growing stronger every day. Jose and Hilda had become irritable, domineering authority figures who were impatient with our (perceived) rebelliousness. Maybe it was the strain of running a church and keeping it afloat or, more likely, it was simply absolute power corrupting absolutely. Either way, it was becoming abundantly clear that we needed to part ways.

Around this time, as Missy and I grappled with our decision, I remember Glenn visiting. He sat and listened patiently as I vented my frustrations about the mind control that we were chafing against. When I was done, he agreed that it was probably best that we moved on. It was obvious that we had thought and prayed about it for quite a long time. This was no irrational, knee-jerk reaction. He admitted that Hilda would be angry with us but urged us to follow our hearts.

Later, after Missy and I had been attending another church for months, Glenn stopped by to confide in us that he was also leaving the Prophet's Guild. Apparently Hilda and Jose had been begging for more and more money from the congregation, claiming they couldn't pay their bills. Strangely enough, Glenn noticed, all kinds of fancy furniture and automobiles were appearing at their residence. When he politely but firmly asked the Arroyos about this glaring discrepancy, it was quite the ugly confrontation. I can't recall whether he was asked to leave or if he decided it was best on his own but Glenn was classier about it than I probably would've been at the time. He at least met with them in private. I was so pissed about their bullshit that I would have stood up in the middle of collection plate time to shout out an inventory of luxury items accumulating at their pastoral palace.

*

Years later, after Missy and I had moved far away from my hometown, my mother called to tell me that Hilda had persuaded her congregation to arrange a mini parade for her down the main drag of Willard. Supposedly God had spoken to her in a vision and revealed that His prophet must be carried in a white buggy pulled by white horses. How the members of the Prophet's Guild didn't balk at this insanity is a mystery to me but, of course, cult members have been persuaded to do more bizarre things than this, and Hilda's cultists eventually were. The entire congregation packed up and relocated to Texas, all according to Yahweh's direct orders, apparently.

Missy and I joked that magic Kool-Aid was soon to follow, but our gallows humor was only thinly disguised pity and sadness for the brainwashed folks involved. After all, most of the Prophet's Guild's members were sweet, sincere outcasts who'd been manipulated by a power-mad husband and wife duo. We knew because we'd once been under their spell. It could very well have been us had the exodus occurred earlier.

A recent internet search for the Arroyos revealed that Hilda (with or without Jose) is still running a cult today, but she's set up shop in Louisiana. I'm guessing this gypsy-like relocation must become necessary once the locals become wise to her snake oil saleswoman's tricks. If I were still a praying man I'd ask the Big Guy to keep Hilda's flock safe from harm, but all I can do is hope that her sleeping sheep wake up before it's too late.

Chapter 31

After the Rock Force gig, Critical Dispatch had the biggest show of our career: Rockfest 1991 in Virginia, playing on the same bill with LaGuardia, the Newsboys, Margaret Becker and Mylon LeFevre! Again, I have no clue how we landed this show, since we were the only unsigned band, but it was a lucky break that we weren't turning down.

On the day of our departure, the band swung into the Missler's Super Valu parking lot to pick me up after a long night of stocking shelves. I was completely exhausted but incredibly psyched about the possibility of playing for thousands of people. By the time we finally rolled into our hotel's parking lot, Darren was driving. Like most places, this fine establishment had an awning over the check-in lane to protect weary travelers from the elements while heaving luggage toward the front doors. Most of us were dozing, staring exhaustedly into space, or talking so our rhythm guitarist had no one to consult and was forced to make an executive decision to pull the RV under the awning so we could check in.

BIG mistake!

We may not have been paying attention *before* this but we were all ears and eyes when an earth-shattering CRUNCH and SCREEEEEEEECH came from just above our heads. "Woah!" Darren slammed on the brakes and, within milliseconds, we were having an impromptu band meeting in the Critical Dispatchmobile's cockpit.

"What's going on?" Gill asked, eyes wide with terror.

"Yeah, what happened?" James redundantly inquired.

Darren was panic-stricken and nearly catatonic. When he was finally able to respond he squeaked, "We're stuck...under the awning. I...I thought there was enough clearance! Oh God! We're dead!"

Before any of us could brainstorm possible solutions for the dilemma, a red-faced hotel manager sprinted up to the driver's side door. It looked like the poor man was utilizing a Herculean amount of self-restraint as he, instead of screaming a litany of homicidal threats, gasped, "What're y'all doin'?!"

"W-we're stuck, sir," Darren yelped. "I thought we could fit."

The manger heaved a heavy sigh, backed up a few steps, scraped his forearm across his sweaty brow, and looked up wearily at his desecrated awning. Then he walked around the RV, gauging the situation and desperately (no doubt) scrambling for a solution that would keep him gainfully employed.

Darren shoved his mulleted head out the window and whined, "Sir...sir? What do you want me to do? I mean, we're halfway through. Do you want me to back up or just try to keep going?"

Silence.

Several of us were brave enough to engage in short, furtive whispering fits but it was mostly quiet enough to hear chicken cooking three miles away. *Was this guy going to call the cops? Would we be locked up? Would we be out of jail in time to play the show? Did southern felons find longhaired Yanks attractive?!*

Oh no! WE'RE ALL GOING TO LOSE OUR ASSHOLE CHERRIES!

Finally, after we'd sweated gallons of Mountain Dew onto the RV's filthy carpet, Manager Man came back to Darren's window. "Well, y'all, I guess the only thing to do is keep goin' forward...SLOWLY. Okay? Just ease it on out from under."

Darren looked nervously from the manager's face to ours, eyes bugging out like a pug on crack. "You sure?" he asked the manager.

Looking like he was about as sure of this course of action as he was that we were some band of rocket scientists, Manager Man sighed, "Yeah, go ahead. But go SLOW!" After issuing his final proclamation on the matter, he backed about twenty yards away. Once he was in a position to eyeball both the top of the awning and the idiots who were carving up its underbelly, he signaled for Darren to proceed.

Shaking his head, our intrepid guitarist mumbled, "Just remember: you told me to do this. If this thing comes down it ain't my fault." As his trembling hand pulled the shifter into gear the rest of us cowered in the back with our beady eyes aimed at the heavens. Not only were we watching the RV's roof, we were all whispering fervent prayers, promising God all kinds of special favors if He somehow got us out of this without massive consequences. "Alright," Darren said. "Here we go."

RRRRRRRRRRRRR.

The engine was straining but there was no forward movement. Darren looked askance to Manager Man who nodded for more aggressive gas pedal action.

RRRRRRRRRRRRRRRRRRRRRRRR.

Nothing. Again, the nod was given for more power. Darren's head shook nervously and looked on the verge of tears.

RRRRRRRRRRRRRRRRRRRRRRRRRRRRRRRRRRRRRRRRRSCRE EEEEEEEEEEEEEEEEECH!

Manager Man winced but waved us onward. As the RV slowly inched forward we all clenched our sphincters and ground our teeth. The horrific racket of metal grinding on metal sounded like Satan using a rusty junkyard crane claw to remove a steel girder from a demon's infected urethra.

SCREEEEEEEEEEEEEEEEEEEEEEEEEEEEEEEEEEEEEEEE
EEEEEEEEEEEEEEEEECRUNNNNNNNNNNNNNNNNNNNNNN
NNNNNNNNNNNNNNCH! THUMP! THUMP! THUMP!

And, like the evil spirits Christ cast out of a man and into some swine (that promptly drowned themselves), we were out of one mess only to wallow in another.

*

After we parked and did the walk of shame into the hotel lobby, the manager informed us that we'd be receiving a bill for damages incurred as soon as he could get an estimate from a contractor. You'd think that hearing this would've dampened our spirits but, NO. We just checked in, found our rooms, and proceeded to jump up and down on our beds like elementary kids on a sugar high. *Time to celebrate! We're playing at a huge rock festival!*

Ah, the ignorance and lack of foresight that comes with youth. If this happened today I'd worry myself sick about where all of that money would come from. Of course, youth and naiveté aren't the only factors to blame here. James was at least a decade older than the rest of us and he wasn't exactly having a meltdown over this either. Maybe he was just being a stoic leader and keeping his financial worries bottled up to avoid distracting us before our big show.

220

We *did* have the biggest gig of our careers to focus on, but let's not dismiss the typical Christian mindset's impact. What do I mean? Well, if you go around believing that you've been claimed as the Bride of Christ and that His angels watch over you, then it's easy to become a little reckless. It's easy to revert to a teenager's mentality of, *Yeah, I just made a mess here, but Mom and Dad will be along with a broom and dustpan to clean it up.* This worldview is even more distressing when Daddy is omnipotent and forgiving. All you gotta do is beg for forgiveness and plead for Abba Father to use His holy Houdini magic to make it all better.

As long as there aren't any random events that cause you to get your ass in a bind after invoking this prayer, then you won't question whether Yahweh always has your back. Unfortunately, though, most Christians tend to wear permanent faith blinders that don't allow physical evidence to disrupt their beliefs. As long as a believer's been indoctrinated with enough conflicting scripture to cover both the good and evil in life, there's no danger of reality rearing its ugly head.

For example, let's say I was driving along, rocking out to some righteous Christian metal, and began speeding without realizing it. Suddenly there are cop cruiser lights in my rearview and I'm being signaled to pull over. This is where the I Made a Boo-Boo supplication begins, with two possible results:

1. I'm cited with a traffic violation: *Oh, God didn't keep me from getting that speeding ticket when I begged Him to get me off the hook. He must've been teaching me a lesson about obeying the law of the land. I'm such a dirty heathen who's undeserving of His grace. Please forgive me!*

Or:

2. I'm given a warning and let off the hook: *Whew! Thank you, Lord! Praise Jesus! I know I totally deserved that speeding ticket but you saved me. I'm not worthy but I promise to never do it again and I'll read my Bible every day from now on!*

Do you see how this brainwashed state insulates the faithful from personal responsibility? Sure, Catholics have the "drink like fishes all week then repent on Sunday" stereotype but most of the mackerel snappers I know aren't so immersed in their personal relationship with Christ that they don't hold themselves responsible. In fact, they're usually brought up to feel obsessively guilty for their actions, unlike many born again folks.

So it was quite easy for all of us to go from shitting ourselves over that awning to bouncing like toddlers on our hotel beds. There *was* the threat of a massive repair bill, but either way Jehovah Jireh was our provider and his grace was sufficient. *Worry? Why? Dude, it's water off a duck's back!* The Blood of the Lamb washed our inhibitions away.

Yet, as an atheist I've been subjected to countless attacks about my supposed lack of a moral foundation. Such verbal barrages often sound like this: "If you don't believe in God then what's to stop you from going out and raping and pillaging like savages? You have no moral compass without the Bible. There's no way you can know right from wrong!"

Oh, wait, didn't God command the Israelites (Deuteronomy 20:10-14) to kill their enemies' men and then take any of their livestock, children and women as spoils of war? Did they adopt the children and put the livestock out to pasture while courting the ladies like gentleman? I'm COMPLETELY sure all of those widows and virgins, grieving for their murdered fathers, brothers, and husbands, were just LEAPING at the chance to get remarried and pop out some Hebrew babies. "Oooh! Thanks for making me a widow. That's SO hot! Take me NOW, stud. My loins are aching for your circumcised shmekele!"

Anyway, the wrecked awning situation was one of those lucky times when our idiotic lack of concern happened to jive with events that didn't force us to face the repercussions of our actions. You see, when the promoter for the festival took us to the venue, we relayed the details of our dilemma. As luck would have it, he was a construction supervisor (What are the odds?) so he whipped up an estimate and brought a crew out to patch things up.

Of course we interpreted this as God providing an answer to our prayers, but I've had many similarly happy resolutions to self-inflicted problems as an atheist. For example, two months ago I tried to fix one of my ancient work car's passenger doors that wasn't staying closed. When I couldn't figure out what the problem was, I looked at the driver's side door latch to see what was different about the properly functioning part. Being the mechanically DEclined geek that I am, I poked around with a screwdriver over and over until I fucked up the one good latch of the two. So, for a few days I had to drive to work with my doors being held closed by bungee cords while chanting the humble mantra of, "Please don't let me get pulled over! Please don't let me get pulled over!" My friends, you haven't lived until you've experienced the adrenaline rush of car doors flapping like hummingbird wings as you careen down back roads at sixty miles per hour!

Anyway, the Auto Collision Repair teacher I work with was able to fix the driver's side door, but no parts could be found for the passenger side. The next morning I arrived at work, ripped off the previous day's page from my People of Wal-

Mart.com desktop calendar, and POW! There it was: the solution to my dilemma. Just when I had begun to panic and wonder where the money for a different work car would come from, a humiliating photo of a redneck's hillbilly truck door repair job sparked an epiphany. Grinning and laughing like a loon, I ran off to show the Auto Collision Repair teacher, who shook his head in mock disgust before assuring me that he could indeed bolt a nine inch barrel bolt to my car door to hold it shut.

Hallelujah!

Saved by white trash ingenuity!

The only difference between the religious Stephen and the atheist Stephen is that now my brain isn't imposing a Christian worldview's patterns on the events that I experience. My grey matter doesn't have to squeeze a bunch of random occurrences into a dogmatic, church-approved formula in order to praise Yahweh (or avoid having a crisis of faith as the shit hits the fan) for the chaos of everyday existence. Instead of thanking a higher power when life is good, I'm simply thankful that (occasionally) things turn out in my favor instead of life squatting over me and unleashing a constant barrage of nuclear diarrhea down on my head.

*

We were the first band to play at the festival, which was fitting since we didn't have a record in the shops. As we set up our gear on that warm, sunny morning, an army of men swarmed around us to mike our amps. We were used to gruff northerners who barked at us to turn our amps down or hit the drums harder so it came as a shock that, as I strapped on and plugged my bass guitar into my amp (with shaking hands) a ninja with a southern accent popped up from behind my Ampeg mini-stack (which was being paid for with a personal loan) and said, "Excuse me, sir. Would you mind if I ran a microphone cable from your amp head into the sound system?"

As if the culture shock of being on a stage that huge wasn't enough to freak me out, this southerner's ridiculously polite hospitality unnerved me to the nth degree. I think I stood gaping for a few seconds at the insanity of his etiquette before being able to respond with, "Uh, um, yeah. Sure." Somehow he managed to avoid looking at me like I was mentally handicapped.

When we took the stage there were only a thousand or so spectators to watch our set, which was a *massive letdown* compared to the usual ten to one hundred we normally played for. I was so tense that I didn't play very well at all. It wasn't that I made mistakes *constantly* but the stage fright made it impossible to really get into a groove and let the music envelop me. At one point, right after I'd managed to miss a note or two due to my trembling hands and rattled psyche, I looked offstage and saw several members of LaGuardia, musical heroes of ours, watching us. I jerked my head back to my fretboard as even more adrenaline shot through my quivering frame. *Oh my God! Tony Castle and David Chopin are over there watching. I'd better headbang and rock out more or they'll think I'm half-assing it!*

We managed to finish our seven songs without humiliating ourselves and with some (polite?) applause that seemed to grow in intensity. After we hustled our gear into the wings and locked it up in the U-Haul, it was time to run our assigned merch table. None of us were feeling too cocky after that tentative performance so we weren't sure if anyone would want to meet or greet us, let alone cough up some cash for a t-shirt or cassette. Luckily a decent amount of folks did, which kept us from feeling like the ugliest girls at the dance.

Before leaving James insisted that we hunt down the promoter and insist on being paid. At the time I thought this was being a tad pushy (especially considering how he bailed us out of Awning Gate) but it turned out to be a very smart move. He paid us our contracted fee, $100 or so, and we split.

Later, we found out that virtually *none* of the other acts were paid. To this day I wonder if any of them heard that the lowly, unsigned band from Ohio was paid but they weren't. There were plenty of people in the crowd as the day went on so I'm not sure what happened with the money. Perhaps the promoter spent too much on advertising or maybe the ticket prices weren't high enough. Either way, the signed artists had to have been paid a certain percentage up front to even show up so, along with their merch sales, most could have broken even.

Still, this tended to be better than the norm in the Christian music industry. People would go out on tour, leaving their families behind, surviving on borrowed tour support money from their record labels. Band members lived on roughly $200 per week (in the early nineties) and then had to find jobs when they came home. If they didn't sell enough cassettes or CDs to pay back the tour support loans, then they ended up in debt for the privilege of spreading the Gospel. Meanwhile, the fat cats at their record label lounged around in luxurious offices that were almost as nice as their secular counterparts' digs. Granted, this wasn't any different from the secular music industry, but shouldn't it have been? Maybe I was naïve, but I sure thought it was supposed to be more Christ-like than that.

*

Somewhere along the way home, probably in Kentucky, we stopped for gas. While we filled up, stretched our legs and grabbed snacks, a beat up clunker came lurching into the parking lot with black, oily smoke billowing from under its hood. Even a mechanically declined dork like me could tell something was seriously wrong as this ancient sedan heaved and stalled just before reaching a parking spot. A very bedraggled, middle-aged southern woman and her six or seven year-old son exited, looking as forlorn as any two humans could.

Since Darren was a grizzled veteran of car problems he went over to offer assistance. After a few minutes our intrepid rhythm guitarist came back toward the station with an empty plastic jug. "That lady's car overheated big time. It was so hot its oil was burning. I'm gonna go get some water." We stood there gaping like idiots so he had to spell out what decent people should be doing at a time like this. "Can you guys go talk to her? She seems pretty upset."

Apparently this woman, we'll call her Joan, had been driving around the hills of Kentucky after escaping from her abusive, drunkard husband. Joan was a backslidden Christian who had gotten drunk, grabbed her six year-old son Harvey, and went out in search of a cliff to use as a suicidal exit ramp from the hell she called life. Fortunately her piece of shit car had other plans.

Unfortunately, for Joan, these circumstances washed her up on the same shore as six idiots in a Christian rock band. As Darren tended to her automobile's needs, under the watchful eyes of Harvey, we gathered around Joan to preach the gospel. She politely told us that she believed in God but hadn't been to church in a while. Then she called to her son, "Harvey, come on over and meet these boys."

Eyes wide with concern, the boy exclaimed, "But, Momma, them's longhairs!"

"Harvey! Come here." Joan sounded desperate for any diversion that might derail our preaching. "Don't be afraid. They're good Christian boys like you!"

Harvey still looked quite skeptical, but he wandered over and let us introduce ourselves. He even chimed in to explain that his momma's "church house was alright but it got awful loud and scary sometimes!"

Joan just smiled, her face weary and tear-stained, and explained to her son, "That's just how people get when they love the Lord."

This whole exchange lightened the mood for a bit, but the conversation eventually circled back to Joan's horrible mission that failed. Understandably, she felt terrible for what she'd almost done. In the end we convinced her that God had caused the car failure that saved their lives and she needed to pray the salvation prayer with us. With Joan's rededication to Jesus achieved, we all hugged and said goodbye.

Some details of our conversation with Joan and Harvey are hazy. I wish I could recall whether she was going back to her psycho husband or planning to start anew. Hopefully none of us urged her to try and patch things up with that asshole and, if we did, I can only count on her being wise enough to disregard some well-meaning Yanks' naïve advice.

But I do remember all of us longhairs praising God on the way home for using us to stop Joan's suicide and help halt her backslide. *We are not worthy,* we prayed, *to be used as your vessels, Lord, but thank you for choosing us anyway! Thank you for showing your mercy through these circumstances.*

In reality, given Joan's religious upbringing and the circumstances of that fateful evening, we really had nothing to do with her choice. After that car broke down, her mind had already found a religious way to explain it. Everything she'd ever been taught as a Christian child and adult, along with the her motherly guilt as she witnessed the mortal terror in her son's eyes during her drunken suicide attempt, predestined that she'd see that automobile's noxious, black smoke as divine intervention. We only provided confirmation for what she'd already decided.

The main thing that bothers me about this incident is our lack of follow through. Anyone with common sense would have gotten Joan's contact information in order to steer her toward domestic violence and mental health counseling. Yes, our hearts were in the right place but we were ill-equipped to truly help in situations like this. Sadly, this never even occurred to us and, I'm sure, most other rock evangelists.

Chapter 32

Once again, after fleeing from Jose and Hilda's cult, Missy and I were without a church home, but the Prophet's Guild era had left us with bandaged wounds that were infected with skepticism. Instead of leaping into the first congregation that seemed inviting, we found ourselves lurking in the back pews, carefully assessing the situation and looking for warning signs. Did the preacher appear manipulative? Were the people in the sanctuary being conned out of their time and money? Was the doctrine sound or were unhinged interpretations of scripture being presented?

Still, this newfound caution only helped to partially protect us. Our spiritually burned out selves remained vulnerable because we still felt an over-exaggerated sense of duty to the church. If we didn't at least visit *some* kind of church for spiritual nourishment then, clearly, we were backsliding into heathendom.

To assuage my guilt over this I spent extra time studying the Bible every night. If work and day-to-day responsibilities prevented this, my conscience practically flayed me alive. *Jesus suffered and died for my sins on the cross, forsaking His father's heavenly kingdom to redeem my sorry hide, and this is how I repay Him? I can't even manage to read a few chapters of the Bible and meditate on them? Praying for family and friends is too much of a burden, you self-centered jerk?*

Yet, in the midst all of this self-loathing, I had no desire to leap back into the rank and file of God's Army. I felt so disillusioned, used, and betrayed. What if I got involved in another seemingly upright crusade that careened down the path to Looneyville? How could I trust any preacher to have my best interests at heart? How could I know if my tithe money wasn't being used to line the pockets of another megalomaniac? And, most importantly, how could I trust my own judgment on these matters since I was so incredibly wrong about the Prophet's Guild?

*

There was, however, one great side effect of our newfound distaste for blind allegiance to the church: Missy and I began to develop an Us Against the World attitude. We didn't know whom we could trust, other than each other, so we became closer than we'd been in years.

Realizing how suffocating the Arroyos' hold had been allowed me to see that Missy didn't need me to be a watchdog over her faith. Gradually, with plenty of missteps along the way, I learned to stop being a control freak and start being a true husband.

Hell, we even starting buying SECULAR CDs and listening to them together!

Crazy, right?

*

Around this time, Cole, the lead singer of Critical Dispatch, started attending the Church of God of Prophecy. He kept raving at band practice about how cool and laid back the preacher was. This pastor, we'll call him Pete, was really nonthreatening, according to Cole, and as a bonus, he played a mean piano and sang like a powerful, black gospel singer, even though he was a pasty white, nerdy, freckly ginger from New Mexico.

I was intrigued and, noncommittally, agreed to visit. As Cole promised, no one pounced on me and prophesied over me on my first visit. Pastor Pete didn't slobber on me while telling me that God had a special plan for my life. He simply played the hell out of his piano and sang like his soul was going to explode through the roof of his skull, which gave me goose bumps. His sermon was decent, even if it was heavy on emotion and light on substance and, after the service, Pete didn't pressure me to come back; he just shook my hand and said it was nice to meet me. I wasn't overly blown away by the place, but I also was wise enough to attribute this to my jadedness. Even the most amazing church on the planet would've had to grow on me like a fungus after that Prophet's Guild fiasco.

Two weeks later I visited again. It was tempting to come back before that but doing so was comparable to appearing desperate by calling a girl the day after a good date. So this pattern of biweekly attendance continued for a few months until, before I knew it, I'd become a regular. After seeing that my reconnaissance had confirmed the Church of God of Prophecy's tentative acceptableness Missy started tagging along. We weren't exactly sprinting to the altar and asking how to sign up as full time members, but we were there.

Still, it didn't take long before the pressure to get involved started. Pete wanted a full praise and worship band but he already had a bass player so I was asked to have a go at playing drums. Pete tutored me on some percussion basics and, before I knew it, even though I had zero confidence in my abilities, the Church of God of Prophecy had a new drummer. Each week Pete would patiently teach me a painfully simple beat for the songs and I'd rock it out in front of the congregation on Sunday with the precision of a Sumo wrestler dancing ballet. Over time my skills improved, which was encouraging, but this only lead to Pete suffering from the delusion that this Hines guy could branch out into intense, syncopated rhythms and fancy drum fills. Sadly, much like any algebraic equations I've labored over, any attempts at improvisation lead to catastrophic derailments, which eventually killed my confidence.

Pete also started working to get me involved with other church activities. As is usually the case with any organization, most people want to reap the benefits but few are willing to do the work. Everyone wanted amazing music but nobody wanted to commit to the band. All of the parents expected fantastic Sunday school lessons for their youngins but no one signed up to teach them. So, once our faithful pastor found out that I'd taken a few education courses in college, the pressure was on. I reluctantly agreed, after weeks of Pete's begging, to teach the middle school/junior class, but only on a trial basis.

I was terrified about bombing with the kids and confided in Pete about it. "I can't do this! What am I supposed to teach about?" I whined.

"You can do it," he assured me. "Just remember that they're trying real hard to be grownups but they still desperately want to be little kids at the same time. Just have fun."

"Okay, but, will you sit in on my lesson for at least a little while? Just to make sure I don't screw up?"

Pete agreed and was true to his word. My lesson was received with as much enthusiasm as any group of sleepy eleven to fourteen year olds can muster. And, since the hooligans didn't duct tape me to a chair and shoot spit wads at my face, Pete was convinced that I was a natural. The job was mine.

While all of this was going on, Missy was roped into running Children's Church (AKA: Babysit Our Brats So We Can Get Away From Them!). Once again, nobody else wanted to do it and, although we had no kids of our own, my wife was guilt tripped into rugrat duty. To make matters worse I, feeling a lot of peer pressure from the congregation, urged her to try to stick it out. She tolerated all of this nonsense for a while, but Missy is anything but a wilting flower. After being bit by several of the little demon-possessed brats she decided that she'd had more than enough of being told, "Nobody else will do it. You have to. We can't have them in there unattended!" and finally she informed the parents that this wasn't *her* problem and *they* could find someone else. Of course this meant that the old biddies and soccer moms of the congregation treated Missy like a selfish piece of shit, even though none of their lazy asses were willing to share the burden.

*

Now, I'm not the sharpest tool in the crayon box, but my increasingly pathetic attempts at percussion and teaching Sunday school eventually lead to an epiphany. *Why am I doing all of these things?* I asked myself. *Is it because I enjoy them? Or is it because I feel OBLIGATED to do them? Are these duties being performed out of love or guilt?* I knew the answer before I even asked myself these questions.

Obviously I was burned out. There was nothing left to do but wipe my slate clean at the Church of God of Prophecy and see what happened. So I asked to be relieved of my duties. It was easiest to give up the Sunday school gig. I had no trouble coming up with lessons and the kids didn't despise me, but I couldn't help feeling incredibly guilty for forcing them to sit through a lesson on one of the only two days they weren't obligated to learn something. Weren't they having enough adult wisdom crammed down their throats? Would I have wanted more classes and learning activities over the weekends when I was their age?

HELL no!

As for the drumming, my screw-ups were outnumbering my successes but music was still my passion. However, I knew that, if I kept one foot in that doorway it would only be a matter of time before other jobs were slipped onto my plate. Pete understood but his acceptance of my resignations was reluctant at best. I felt bad for sticking him with more vacancies to fill but my mind was made up. There was no backing out now, no matter how much his puppy dog eyes begged and pleaded.

Not long after this, while leaving the Church of God of Prophecy after a Sunday morning service, I found a newsletter under my car's windshield wiper blade. It was some kind of Christian reading material so I chucked it in the car to peruse later. Little did I know that this little periodical was a breadcrumb that would lead me to the last church I'd ever attend.

Chapter 33

The next big gig on Critical Dispatch's schedule, playing for the youth group at the so-uptight-our-assholes-whistle "Onward-Christian-Soldiers" Christian Alliance Church in Willard, was booked by our new manager, Earl. Earl was a spoiled brat momma's pretty boy who was quite the con man. He had zero experience in representing musicians but his smooth-talking abilities had always enabled him to slide into many positions for which he had no training. Originally he'd auditioned to be our singer (before we found Cole) and, since he couldn't compensate for his lousy singing with bullshit, he hung around until he could slither on board as our manager, a job for which bullshitting was essential.

Anyway, the Christian Alliance's congregation went nuclear once flyers advertising our concert began circulating. *Who in the world were these wolves in sheep's clothing? We can't have longhaired heavy metal types desecrating our sanctuary and leading our young folk astray! Dear God, NO!*

The painfully white bread Alliance members objected to everything about us: our hair length, ripped jeans, sleeveless t-shirts, distorted guitars, screaming vocals, drum beats...even the fact that we were *selling tickets* to get into the show. We had to have Pastor Scott from Victory Christian Fellowship (with whom we had regular counseling sessions) write a letter of recommendation, vouching for the authenticity of our walk with Christ, to the Alliance's pastor to calm some nerves. From there the freaked-out-flock had to be further mollified by a long epistle (from their assistant pastor) that listed specific details about the number of young people who'd been lead to Christ at our recent shows as well as information about how we followed up with these kids to ensure they were nurtured in the faith. [We completely fabricated the facts about our supposed follow-up ministry and somehow convinced ourselves that it was true. We *never* took the time to check in on converts unless they showed up to watch us rehearse.] The Alliance's pastor even forced us to change the flyers to say that there was a SUGGESTED two dollar donation to get in, not a required ticket purchase. Never mind the fact that any real concert required a ticket bought with real paid admission!

To make matters even worse, as we were trying to put out these fires to move the show forward, Gill announced that he was leaving the band. This came as quite a shock, especially since he was one of the two main songwriters in the band. At the time he claimed that he'd prayed about it and felt that God was telling him to move on, but he later admitted that his relationship with James had soured. Gill had recently gotten very serious with his girlfriend and was spending a lot of time driving to her home in Michigan. This didn't sit well with James because it became impossible to keep an eye on our lanky lead guitarist to make sure he wasn't fornicating.

Of course, our guru/keyboardist never phrased it that way. Instead, James initially tried guilt tripping Gill for his flagging dedication to the Critical Dispatch cause: "How can we write songs together if you're either working or in Michigan? I miss you, man. You're my brother!" When this technique didn't work, the pleading turned to angry, barbed, self-righteous accusations about Gill's salvation being in jeopardy. The rest of us didn't even know this was happening so, by the time we heard we had a core member to replace, there was no talking Gill out of it. He'd had enough of James trying to be his second father/cult leader and it was a miracle that he was even willing to stick around long enough for us to find a replacement.

*

We cast our nets far and wide with classified ads for a "committed, born-again lead guitarist for a metal band" and the fish they brought in were truly strange. Some could barely play rhythm guitar, let alone lead. Most of them didn't have a single musical influence in common with us, which was a massive problem.

Eventually, after auditioning everyone under the Son (including a geriatric hippy with a Hendrix fixation) a young man in his early twenties, we'll call him Frank, got the gig. He drove over ninety minutes to try out which, along with his guitar playing, floored us. Frank's original riffs sounded scarily like our own and he played lead like a man possessed. Hell, he'd even routed out his guitar's neck between frets so he could play faster, like his hero: George Lynch from Dokken.

After we'd jammed together there was the requisite interview to see if his faith seemed genuine. Frank assured us that he was a bonafide believer who had no problem driving all the way from Canal Fulton, OH to Willard twice a week for practice. We were so enamored with this guy that, as we later admitted to ourselves, we ignored our gut feeling that he was faking his faith in order to be in the group. He did admit that he was a smoker who was praying for the strength to quit, so that scored some brownie points with James and Darren, who battled with this addiction as well.

Gill was true to his word and showed up as often as possible to teach our tunes to Frank. Darren helped but he often played different parts so there was only so much he could do. Still, it didn't take long for the veteran members of Critical Dispatch to notice our new guitarist's distant attitude and cocky demeanor. He wasn't very friendly and didn't joke around much, but we hoped he'd loosen up with time. To make matters worse, he'd shrug off his frequent mistakes at band practice by curtly stating, "Yeah, whatever. I'll have it down by next week."

Unfortunately, this promised improvement never happened since Frank wasn't the fastest learner and, as our gig at the Willard Christian Alliance Church loomed on the horizon, we had a decision to make. Should we cancel this show that had been so difficult to book? Maybe all of the Alliance's objections to hosting us, along with Frank's struggles with our material, were signs that God didn't want this concert to go forward. Or should we persevere? It *was* possible that God was testing our dedication with adversity. Wouldn't the Lord want us to play gigs to avoid defaulting on our PA and RV loans?

To avoid looking like the incompetent douches that the church's elders assumed we were, James came up with the idea of having Gill play most of the set. Then, when we were down to the final seven songs, Frank would be introduced as our next axe man, play two tunes with Gill and Darren, then Gill would bow out for the remainder of the show. In retrospect, this was a genius way to cover our asses for choosing a guitarist who was already showing telltale signs of being a very poor choice.

*

On the night of the Alliance gig, we were all, justifiably, on edge. Before we could leave to set up our instruments and PA,

Frank called to say he was running late. We all bit our tongues and pretended that this guy wasn't pissing us off. Then, he *still* wasn't there when it was time to soundcheck. Grumbling within the Critical Dispatch camp increased. After soundcheck we all went home to shower then came back to slide into our fancy (now mostly denim and leather) stage clothes. Frank STILL hadn't arrived. Now we were REALLY getting pissy. Yeah, Gill still knew all the songs and could do the show without a hitch, but we'd already printed posters promising a dramatic unveiling of our newest member. What if this guy didn't show?

As our advertised stage time loomed closer and closer, we took turns prowling the church's lobby, greeting friends, family, and fans while nervously looking around for Frank every millisecond or two. Of course, everyone pretended to be fooled by our happy go lucky pre-show banter, except for our wives and girlfriends. Missy instantly knew something was up. "Are you okay? Is something wrong?" she inquired.

After pulling her aside I whispered, "Frank STILL isn't here! We go on in ten minutes! He still needs to load in his gear, tune, and soundcheck. We're SCREWED!"

"It'll be okay," my ever-supportive spouse assured me. "Try to calm down. He'll be here."

I rolled my eyes, shook my head, and stalked off. Of course, as soon as I began stomping away, I caught sight of our wayward guitarist out of the corner of my eye. "Frank! You made it!"

Being the arrogant little ass that he was, Frank showed no indication of remorse or the need thereof. "Hey," he smirked. "Where do I set up?"

Being the hardass that *I* was, my angst-ridden, pasty face burst into a relieved smile as I pointed to the church's sanctuary like a stooge, instantly hating myself for not giving the jerk the tongue lashing he so richly deserved.

When the others were informed that Frank had FINALLY arrived there were plenty of sarcastic comments and promises about letting the newbie know that Critical Dispatch didn't operate this way, but I don't remember anyone actually following through with it. Instead, the show proceeded as planned. Gill played his part of the set. Frank was introduced. An altar call was answered by an apparently satisfactory (for the Alliance's church elders) number of heathens, and we all lived happily ever after.

That is, until we watched the videotape of the concert.

Begin Sarcastic Side Note:

You see, Critical Dispatch just LOVED watching ourselves on tape. We never admitted to it because we *claimed* the footage was being studied to improve our stage show. SURE it was! By the time we'd been around for a couple of years, each member had a fully stocked VHS library of C.D. concerts and rehearsals. Any time a camera was aimed at us, we hammed it up and soaked up the delusion that we were rock stars on the rise. But this behavior was *never* motivated by vanity or a desperate need for the spotlight. No no no no NO! We were just smashing the stereotype of boring, baptized in vinegar Christians who never had any fun. By golly *we* knew how to unclench our butt cheeks and live a little! Critical Dispatch put the FUN in fundamentalism, baby!

End Sarcastic Side Note

Upon scrutinizing the audio-visual evidence from the Christian Alliance gig, we all felt like something just wasn't right about Frank's performance but none of us could put a finger on it. Gill saw the footage and, in his typically blunt manner, instantly honed in on the problem: "Whenever he solos he's going in and out of the correct key. He doesn't know his scales." And, sure enough, we fast-forwarded through the show and there were parts of Frank's leads that sounded great and others where he was clearly floundering. Whether this was due to him being too slow and/or lazy to learn the songs properly or, as Gill hypothesized, his ignorance of theory, we knew something had to be done.

At our next practice, we had a band meeting to discuss the issue with Frank. Honestly, I have no memory of how that confrontation went, so it couldn't have gone horribly awry, but it wasn't long before Frank simply stopped showing up and we were back in the market for new axe man.

*

Shortly after Frank's departure, I ran into a legendary local guitarist, we'll call him Julio, at my place of employment. Julio, a Latino, gentle giant of a stoner (until organized religion got a hold of him) had come closer than most in our area to becoming a rock star. When he asked if I was still jamming, I vented about our frustrating search for a new member and I pretended to joke while asking him if he wanted to audition. Julio replied, "Oh, wow, man. I appreciate the offer but I don't know if I'm your guy. I mean, I believe in God and everything but I don't walk the walk like you guys."

"Ahhh, come on, Julio," I said. "We aren't perfect either. Why don't you just come by and jam and have some fun. No pressure." I was becoming quite adept at lying through my teeth while remaining steadfastly in denial that the sin was even occurring. "Stop by on Saturday and we'll have fun."

Julio smiled and, for a harmless hippy, gave me a handshake that could've crushed Arnold Schwarzenegger's paw. "Well thanks, man. I'll think about it and see if I can swing by."

As soon as I made it home from work I called James and told him about the conversation. He, of course, pretended to be apprehensive about Julio's non-born-again condition, but said we should pray for him. Oh, and *of course* we could jam with him. The worst-case scenario would be: we'd have no musical chemistry but God might use us to plant a seed, right?

So Julio came over and rocked out with us. His favorite band was Led Zepplin but his riff and lead style sounded more like Jake E. Lee from Ozzy Osbourne's band (circa the *Bark at the Moon* and *The Ultimate Sin* era). This had us drooling, even before he whipped his guitar up to his face and plucked a solo out with his teeth and tongue. Holy shit stains of St. Stratocaster could that guy play!

Now, I hope this next unprecedented revelation doesn't induce undue coronary distress but, just as we'd done several times in the past, Critical Dispatch applied the full court evangelistic press on another highly coveted heathen musician in order to fill a vacancy. Of course Julio would've been the target of our witnessing efforts anyway. I mean, the fact that he *happened* to shred like a Mexican metal maestro was just God's way of demonstrating divine providence!

To make a pathetic story even more pathetic, Julio (miraculously?) converted and joined the cause. Still, his membership in the C.D. gang was probationary from the beginning. Why? Well, partially because he refused to wear glam clothes or grow his Slash-like hair out again, but mostly because he was living in sin with the mother of his two daughters and had no plans to get married. As far as he was concerned God could see that he was in a faithful, loving relationship, so why would a piece of paper make it any more legit? Didn't people in Biblical times get married without a license from city hall?

Our only creaky philosophical leg to stand on involved how this looked to the rest of the world. Sure, most of us were secretly judging Julio for his stubborn nuptial nonconformity but, if our fans and any potential converts found out, wouldn't they think we were hypocrites? How could we dare tell them to repent if one of our members was openly living in sin? But every time this argument came up Julio would simply shrug and say, "Who are they to judge? God knows my heart. It's nobody else's business." This frustrated the hell out of James but I secretly could find no fault in Julio's logic. All of us fell *far* short of perfection. As long as Julio wasn't cheating on his faithful partner then what was the big deal?

*

Over time we played some low and high profile gigs with Julio. The biggest was a battle of the bands at a Columbus, OH venue called The King's Place, which was THE place for all signed, national Christian rock bands to play in the Buckeye state. So we practiced our asses off, invited all of our friends and family to cheer us on, played one of the best sets of our lives, and lost to a shitty band that *happened* to have two close friends on the judging panel. So much for Christians setting a higher standard than the godless scumbags of the world. It, just like everything else, boiled down to the politics of nepotism.

After that show, Darren left the band to focus on his marriage and new family. Instead of finding a replacement, we decided to interpret this exodus of another founding member as God's way of improving the band. Darren rarely practiced and almost always sounded rusty. No amount of nagging or guilt tripping ever affected his disposition, so why not continue with only one guitarist? Sure, our trademark harmonized guitar parts would disappear, but James could do some of Darren's licks with his keyboard. Plus, many of our heroes managed to still sound massive with only one six-string slinger. Of course, many also used prerecorded backing tracks but, whatever!

At this point we were blind to the band's crumbling foundation because we were on a mission. Why? Well, our favorite Christian rock band, LaGuardia, was soon coming to the area and we wanted to have a fresh tune to play for their main songwriter/guitar player, Tony Castle. So we recorded a demo of our newest song, "Unity", which we'd written right before Gill left, at a local studio. This was the only track I was ever allowed to contribute a significant musical part to because Gill was ever adamant about not being able to write off of a bass line, which frustrated me to no end. So when he had to miss several rehearsals due to working overtime, I seized the opportunity by showing the band the bridge riff I'd written. Everyone loved it and pledged to tell Gill that the new part was cemented in the song, whether *he* liked it or not. Upon returning, he did grumble but it was clear Gill was facing a united front so the riff stayed.

SUCK IT, BASS-O-PHOBE!

When LaGuardia finally rolled into Ohio, we approached Mr. Castle about producing a multi-song demo for him to shop to his record label. After Tony soundchecked, we all piled into LaGuardia's tour van (which may or may not have had several porno magazines on the front seat—I can neither confirm nor deny this) to check out our tune. He listened to it a couple times while we sat, sweating bullets and praying. "Well," he said, turning to look at all of us. "It's a good, catchy song but, stylistically, it's kind of all over the place. You have some bluesy riffs, then an Iron Maiden drum fill, a Gun n' Roses bridge, then a Queensryche-style section before the solo. Plus, the bass player switches from eighth notes to quarter notes in the chorus, which kills the momentum at the most crucial point of the song."

At that very second you could've heard my heart crash through the van's underbelly. One of my musical idols singled me out for humiliation! Son of a biscuit-eating bitch! Of course, being a self-taught musician, I had no clucking flue what eighth or quarter notes were, but...FUCK! Tony had just crucified my bass line in front of my bandmates. While everybody else in C.D. was focused on kissing Tony's ass and agreeing with his every criticism, I was quietly wishing I could die, slither out the side door, or drop kick Castle's man-giblets into the roof of his guitar god mouth.

"But," Tony continued. "This bridge riff is the best part of the song." He rewound the cassette to the section that I contributed and hit play. "I freakin' LOVE this riff! Heck, I'd have no problems using that in a LaGuardia song. What a groove!"

Immediately, my broken heart reassembled, waxed and buffed itself to a heavenly shine, burst back through the van's floor, splatted back into my chest cavity, and pounded out a double bass drum pattern that threatened to shatter my ribcage.

REALLY? He thinks MY riff is the best part of the song? Wow! Holy crap!

Tony popped the cassette out, handed it to James, and said, "If you guys can figure out how to iron out the problems I mentioned, rerecord it, and send it to me then I'd love to produce your demo and shop it to our label."

*

At our next band meeting we shared Tony's feedback with Julio, who politely disagreed. "No disrespect to this Castle guy," he stated quietly. "But I think all the things he disliked about the song are what make it original. It's all of this band's influences mixed together. If you take that stuff out then it's just another formula rock song, man. There are enough of those on the radio already."

Of course, James completely disagreed. "But...I mean, I see your point, Julio, but the only way we're going to get this guy to produce a demo that he'll be proud to pitch to his label is if we do what he says. If Tony says to make it more commercial then we need to do it. When we prove we can sell some CDs *then* we can start deviating from the formula." The word "commercial" was our keyboardist's mantra. If a song wasn't commercial, then it wasn't instantly catchy or worth pursuing. If Tony said we had to beat all of the creative wrinkles out of the track then it was time to start pounding. And something told me that, even if we were signed and proved we could sell albums, James would never allow us to veer from the beaten path of commerciality again.

Initially, all of us agreed with James. I mean, our goal was to get signed to a recording contract, right? So we practically sprinted into the practice room to begin the "Unity" revision process. Julio didn't agree but he bit the bullet and went along with it. First Tom experimented with non-Iron Maiden drum fills. Then I attempted to stick to eighth notes in the chorus. And all of us tried to un-Queensryche the pre-solo section. Naturally, we produced a much stronger song that practically rewrote and rerecorded itself before going on to be the highest grossing crossover hit single in Christian rock/Top 40 history. We were wiping our asses with $100 bills, riding in limos, and turning down groupies who wanted to share carnal knowledge with us.

BAHAHAHAHAHAHAHAHAHAHAHAAHAHAHAHAHAHAHA HAHAHAHAHAHAHAHA!

Actually, every attempt at implementing Mr. Castle's songwriting advice (at best) weakened the song or (at worst) turned it into a derailed train wreck of smoking carnage. Every change sucked the life out of both the tune and our excitement for it. Maybe our imaginations were just too limited to accomplish Tony's vision for "Unity". Perhaps, if we were working side by side with him in a recording studio and he could have supplied concrete suggestions for replacing the offending musical elements, the song could have become commercial.

Or maybe the song was just fine the way it fucking was. To this day, even if the lyrics (and James' Axl Rose style backing vocals in the bridge) make me cringe, I think the song rocks like a mo-fo. It's insanely catchy and has grooves and originality

255

galore. So what if it didn't fit in with the overplayed, music-by-numbers bullshit that dominated the airwaves at the time? So what if it wasn't a safe, sure bet investment for a record company? Since when was rock n' roll EVER supposed to play by the rules of a corrupt establishment? Wasn't it supposed to flip men in suits the bird while pissing on their corporate logo?

DAMN STRAIGHT IT SHOULD!

Eventually we gave up on supposedly improving "Unity" and moved on to writing new songs intended to seduce Castle into producing us, but first we'd have to replace another member.

*

In between writing new tunes, we played some minor gigs that I remember very little about. We sounded great at these shows, but, every time we went back to the rehearsal room, there was zero songwriting chemistry with our new guitarist. His riffs always sounded like classic Zepplin or Pink Floyd, and we were looking for modern hard rock action. James kept saying things like, "That's great, Julio, but, can you make it sound more like Skid Row...or maybe Zakk Wylde?" Of course, this was the equivalent of asking a death metal guitarist to get in touch with his inner bluegrass banjo player. Needless to say, all our songwriting attempts stalled out in gloriously frustrating style.

Plus, several members, most notably James, couldn't stop picking at the scab of Julio's unmarried cohabitation. Every time the subject was brought up, tension mounted and arguments erupted. Eventually, James called a Julio-free band meeting and we voted on whether to issue an ultimatum (get hitched or get ditched!). I don't remember if I was the only one, but I didn't vote for this. Of course, it was still approved with a strong majority.

As if the tension about this was palpable before, the meeting to issue the ultimatum was *the very definition* of tense. Julio restated his belief that God honored his commitment to his woman, with or without the approval of man. James and several others kept beating the holier-than-thou dead horse of "maintaining our integrity in the eyes of the world" we were attempting to evangelize. As voices raised and tempers flared more and more, I shrunk into myself and said less and less. I'd started out trying to defend Julio by asking, "Who are we to judge?" but getting continually shouted down by self-righteous zealots on a witch-hunt killed my fragile confidence. Finally, after hours of this ugly, puritanical exercise in futility, the meeting ended with Julio quitting. I'll never forget his defeated, broken posture as he packed up his gear and left, stating that he didn't want to stay where he wasn't wanted or hold us back in our mission.

That night, I felt so bad about the injustice we'd done that I just couldn't stop thinking about it. For the first time I was embarrassed to be a part of this band I'd helped found. Missy urged me to make my feelings known, so I decided to call Julio to apologize both for my own inaction and the other members' actions.

After at least an hour of deliberation, I had an entire speech rehearsed and ready to go. As soon as Julio answered I planned to launch into an eloquent, heartfelt plea for forgiveness and hopefully he'd be able to at least partially absolve me. Of course, in the typical Stephen Hines style, all plans went out the window as soon as our former guitarist said, "Hello?"

"Hey, Julio." I stammered, choking up and beginning to cry gently, then sobbing like a baby.

"Is this Stephen?" Julio asked.

"Y-yeah."

"Man, you alright? What's wrong?" asked the guy who'd just been unceremoniously scapegoated out of our band. Instead of telling me to never call again and slamming the receiver down hard enough to turn it to dust, Julio instantly went into compassion mode. The concern in his voice just made things a million times worse. Every time I tried to speak my emotions got the best of me, sobbing disintegrating my words into unintelligible gibberish.

Eventually Julio said he'd drive over and pick me up so we could talk things out in person. We ended up riding around in his car with *him* comforting *me* until I'd calmed down enough to converse. In the end he not only accepted my apology, but also thanked me for not jumping on the bandwagon against him. Somehow he didn't even have hard feelings against me, or the band, for the insanity that we put him through. The night ended with Julio and I sharing a manly hug and a promise to stay in touch.

Looking back, I can see that this was the beginning of two huge changes for me: one bad and one good. The negative part would be my hysterical loss of control after a highly emotional situation. Little did I know but this crying fit foreshadowed the arrival of an inherited anxiety disorder. At the time I was twenty-three and, due to complete ignorance about mental illness and the effects of medication for such issues, I wouldn't end up seeking real, professional help for another five years. During that period my reactions to loved ones dying, changing colleges, moving to a new city, and starting a new career would gradually turn me into a neurotic, suicidal mess, which I'll discuss in more detail later.

As for the silver lining of the Julio Incident: this crisis also marked the beginning of my return to a less judgmental outlook on life. After seeing how traumatic a Christian witch hunt can be, I tried harder to accept people for who they were. It's quite easy to stand on a soapbox, hurling hellfire and brimstone sermons at sinners, but being in that room, seeing a grown man pulverized by his so-called friends and brothers, allowed me to witness firsthand the effects of casting stones. It didn't make me feel like I was on the right or superior side of the situation. It made me feel *despicable* and *unclean.* In my heart I knew that Julio's living arrangements weren't sinful, nor were they any of *my* damn business. As long as he and his lady were faithful to each other and did the best they could to grow as lovers and parents, how could anyone in his right mind find fault with that?

Of course, my transformation wasn't immediate. It started with a "hate the sin, not the sinner" mentality and eventually evolved into a "who the hell am I to judge when I'm this fucked up?" attitude. The more instances I witnessed of the church shooting its wounded, along with my growing struggles with anxiety, the less I felt inclined to pounce on people. After all, the list of times I'd fallen short of God's glory would stretch around the planet multiple times. It was becoming clearer and clearer that I had ZERO moral high ground to stand on.

Have I always been able to maintain this enlightened sense of compassion and open-mindedness? No way! Every day I struggle with tolerance toward religious folks (among others) who feel the need to shove their holy book down my throat. When I see news stories about the Westboro Baptist Church holding up "God hates fags!" signs, I lose my shit and scream judgmental obscenities at the TV screen. However, even though I went through an angry, militant atheist stage where I blew up on

260

the faithful both in person and on the internet, I feel I've made progress in the area of empathy.

You want proof?

Okay.

When evangelists from the local Baptist church ring our doorbell and attempt to share the Good News, I don't slam the door after telling them to keep their relationship to themselves. Instead I politely tell them that I'm an atheist and I'd fight for their freedom to believe in God; so I'd also expect them to do the same, at least as far as respecting my right to NOT believe. They usually offer to leave some literature for me to peruse (as a way to get their foot in the door for a return visit) and I just smile and say, "No thank you." If they promise to pray for me then I thank them for that as well. It's taken me years to let go of the bitterness I felt toward organized (and disorganized) religion but I try to remind myself that the Stephen Hines of old engaged in similarly offensive and/or annoying activities. Many were preached at by Brutha Stephen, with or without his merry band of Christian metal evangelists. Perhaps the Baptists, Mormons, and Jehovah's Witnesses who pester me are the female dog named Karma pissing gleefully on my doorstep. It's also possible that the folks who give me shit for being an atheist are also Karma's minions.

Either way, I hope I've paid off my cosmic debt soon so people just leave me the hell alone. Don't they know I'm busy sacrificing goats to Satan and masturbating to midget porn?

SHEESH!

Chapter 34

It took a few days but I finally read that newsletter I'd found on my windshield: issue #1 of *The Idle Babbler Illustrated* by Jeff Priddy. Nothing in it was controversial, but it was intelligent and full of humor. I wrote to the guy and asked to subscribe. He wrote a hilarious letter back, saying he'd put me on his mailing list. I quickly forgot all about it, since I was working full time while, finally, back in college to become an English teacher (I've only been good at two things in life: reading and writing; plus, the only part of my grocery store job I enjoyed was working with teenagers).

But, in a couple months, issue #2 arrived in my mailbox. This issue was deeper and more intellectually challenging, while still as humorous as a great Dave Barry column. So I wrote Mr. Priddy another letter, asking questions and expressing my appreciation for his work.

This cycle of reading and corresponding quickly became a delightful routine and, after writing letters to each other for about a year and a half, we decided to hang out in person for the first time. When he showed up at our apartment, Jeff and I laughed about living less than fifteen miles apart yet there we were writing letters like two old farts. As we sipped cappuccino and chatted, I found out that Jeff had walked away from a cushy post office job to attempt a full time writing career. This intrigued me, obviously, since I dreamed of being an author with no day job. Of course we talked about the Bible quite a bit, too. Before he left we agreed to keep sending letters, just because we enjoyed writing and reading them.

Priddy also sparked a lot of soul searching and questioning with *The Idle Babbler* and his snail mail epistles. It turned out that he was a Universalist who didn't believe that the Bible taught anything about eternal damnation. The verse that was the keystone of his beliefs and teachings was 2 Peter 3:9 (the italics and underlining are my own): "The Lord is not slack concerning *His* promise, as some count slackness, but is longsuffering toward us, not willing that any should perish but that all should come to repentance." To Jeff this was a clear indication that God would and could not fail to save ALL people. I was skeptical but, with each issue of the newsletter, the inconsistencies of mainstream Christian theology became more apparent.

One of my favorites involved the problem of evil. Nothing could exist if God hadn't created it, right? The Devil can't create; destruction is the name of his game. So where did evil come from? God had to have created it since He's omniscient and omnipotent. Bearing this in mind, how could God damn someone to Hell for eternity for falling prey to something He created and introduced to the world? If Yahweh sent Jesus to save us, wouldn't even one person burning forever constitute a colossal failure on His part? To make a long story short, *The Idle Babbler* proved to me, using Bible verses and literal translations of the Greek and Hebrew texts, that all would be saved EVENTUALLY. Some people would have to go through a cleansing process before being admitted to the kingdom which, according to Jeff, wasn't a fluffy cloud palace with angels strumming harps; instead it was an actual paradise on Earth.

Quite a bit of this theory stemmed from the interpretation of the Greek word "aion". Priddy showed his readers how the KJV and NIV bibles, as well as all of the other bestselling translations, sometimes claimed that aion meant an *eternity* while (seemingly at random) other verses maintained that it only indicated a *finite epoch* of time. Of course, most of the verses in which the word eternity was used involved damnation, which makes me wonder how many translators allowed their (or a boss') agenda to influence their choice. Christian scholars have debated over aion for centuries, so this theory isn't new. *The Idle Babbler* just made the information a million times more accessible to non-seminary nerds like me.

I've only studied the issue briefly but I can tell you that orthodox Christians will seriously lose their shit if you take the threat of Hell out of the equation. What's that you say? You require proof? Remember when I mentioned that Critical Dispatch's former lead guitarist, Julio, hadn't been tainted by the self-righteousness that he was subjected to? Well, apparently, word got around the tiny town of Willard, OH that I had (very quietly, mostly so my C.D. bandmates wouldn't find out) become a universalist. So one night my phone rang and it was my old buddy Julio on the other end. Initially I was excited to hear from him and, at first, he made small talk about work, college, and married life; but the conversation swerved unexpectedly to the topic of false religions. Julio claimed that he'd heard rumors of a local "cult" that had brainwashed an old friend. "Can you believe it, man? This dude used to be a rock solid believer, too," he said. And then his tone, as inexplicably as the subject had changed, shifted to that of an angry hellfire and brimstone preacher. "EVERYONE will be saved? That doctrine is a lie of the Devil meant to trick you into hellfire! Why would anyone live a moral lifestyle if everyone gets the same reward in the afterlife? Where's my motivation to be holy if I can just be a filthy sinner and get away with it?" Julio's blistering rant was so rapid fire that I never had a chance to even insert a comment until he was done.

When he *was* finished I played dumb, mumbling and stumbling over my words while acting like I'd never heard about such madness in our community. My change in beliefs was so fresh and new that debating my former bandmate would've been pure folly but, mostly, I was just blindsided and my brain had gone blank.

For a while after Julio's telephonic Kamikaze attack I was very bitter and pissed off toward him. *Who the fuck did he think he was? How dare he call me, insult my intelligence by claiming to talk about some other old friend, then browbeat me with a rabid sermon? He used to be so sweet, calm, and understanding. What the hell happened?*

Oh, yeah.

The CHURCH happened to him.

Where there was once a Live and Let Live hippy there was now an angry, judgmental Pharisee in sheep's clothing. And I helped create that monster. Obviously I wasn't alone. There were plenty of other laypeople and preachers to share the blame but still: how could I continue to carry malice in my heart for Julio when he was clearly imitating what he had seen? Maybe when we forced him out of Critical Dispatch he thought we were some messed up dudes, but now he'd begun to mimic us. We'd not only blasted him with hypocritical attitude but we'd also presented our actions as correct in the eyes of God. Train a child up in the way that he should go, right?

*

In a strange twist of fate, Julio recommended the guitarist, Martin, who ended up replacing him. There aren't many people who would help the band that self-righteously canned them to find a successor, but our former axe man had yet to show any outward signs of being tainted by the Critical Dispatch machine.

Martin, an intelligent pizza deliveryman, was over six-feet tall and about 250 pounds of slovenly guitar prodigy. Everything about this guy was thick and slow, except for his brain and fingers. He even drove an ancient rust bucket boat of a car that floated like an iceberg to and from rehearsals.

On the day of his audition, we had a pow-wow with him to assess his spiritual fitness (can't have another dude shackin' up with a filly!). When James asked him to talk about his theological leanings, Martin sighed heavily, lurched to the side like Jabba the Hut on his couch-throne, and launched into a thick-tongued exegesis on the Name-It-Claim-It doctrine he was studying. He was a member of World Harvest Church (lead by the infamous Pastor Rod Parsley or, as I like to call him, Dick Salad) in Columbus, OH, just like my arrogant boss in the grocery business. This meant that his Bible was full of *proof* that God would bless him with millions and millions of dollars as a reward for being faithful. Thus immediately endearing him to James and making me biased against him. If this guy joined our band would he, like my asshole boss, berate my lack of faith every time I had the sniffles? Would he constantly brag about how he'd need to learn to spell the word "billionaire"? And would he also brag about his church's missionaries refusing to feed starving Africans until they'd listened to a sermon?

Despite my reservations about Martin's arrogance and mega-church membership, his guitar playing blew me away. He not only learned our riffs quickly, he also was able to improvise by adding more advanced chords to them. Plus, every time we made it to a solo section, his Yngwie Malmsteen meets George Lynch fretboard pyrotechnics turned all of us into drooling, grinning imbeciles.

Needless to say, by the end of the jam session he was asked if he wanted to be the newest member of Critical Dispatch. Being the humble, Christlike man that he was, Martin flashed a cocky grin that communicated that his membership was CLEARLY a foregone conclusion and said, "Yeah. I think we can make this work." My gut twisted in warning but it was once again overruled by visions of rock stardom dancing in my head.

*

As rehearsals with Martin began in earnest, we gradually became used to his dry, elitist attitude. If one of us asked him to explain some advanced music theory that he mentioned, he'd roll his eyes before drawling out a condescending quip, implying his shock that we didn't all wear rubber underwear, bite plates, and protective helmets to bed each night. If his ability to have all of the songs down in time for our impending gig was questioned, he'd sigh and snap, "Of COURSE I'll be ready, psssh! These songs aren't hard!" Whenever we couldn't tell if he was joking or making fun of musicians (us) who weren't as blessed with virtuoso ability or Godzilla-sized egos, we laughed and opted to assume the best of him. Clearly we just didn't understand this brother in Christ's sense of humor or personality yet! Or maybe we just needed Martin to keep our egos in check, like the apostle Paul needed that thorn in his side.

For weeks, in spite of how great the band was sounding with Martin on board, there was something bothering me about him. I've never claimed to have the sharpest intellect but I finally figured out what it was: Considering his church affiliation, why in the world he was stuck in a dead end delivery position at a pizza joint? He was six years older than me and a graduate of the World Harvest Bible College. Shouldn't he be preaching alongside his idol, Pastor Parsley, and mopping his fat, sweaty brow with the tithe money of thousands? If his faith and holiness were as great as he claimed, why wasn't Martin being chauffeured to practice in a shiny, black limousine by an elderly manservant who carried and tuned his guitar for him? "No, no, my lord!" Alfred the manservant would exclaim. "Permit *me* to ready your instrument while you dine on fine caviar and smoke Cuban cigars."

My answer and the reason for his lowly economic status became obvious when Martin stayed at my apartment one weekend. Critical Dispatch was practicing on two consecutive days to cram for our new Axe Man's debut gig and, since Martin lived ninety minutes away, my wife and I said he could crash on our couch for one night. After rehearsal I barely had time to eat before shuffling off to my third shift stock crew duties. Missy was working second shift at the time, so Martin was left to his own devices for a few hours. I remember that it felt a little awkward to know that Missy would be alone in our tiny crib with Martin for a few conscious hours before bedtime but I pushed it to the back of my mind because this was a brother in the Lord, after all.

BIG mistake.

After grinding out another eight hours in the crackerstacker salt mine, I came home to find Martin wide-awake. He'd stayed up all night playing his guitar. Since I was completely exhausted from getting virtually no sleep before work, the marital difficulties this posed failed to dawn on me. So, after gorging on some leftovers, I slithered off to bed with my beautiful wife. Obviously, Missy was on a completely different sleep schedule, so she was up and ready to roll in a couple hours. Where was Martin? Sound asleep like a hibernating bear on our sofa.

Needless to say, as the day went on, my wife's attitude became more and more feisty. Missy tried to get things done around the homestead but everything she needed to do might wake the sleeping giant. Our kitchen was a mere ten feet from the sofa so the noisy clattering of dishes being washed wouldn't do. The carpet desperately needed vacuumed (especially since our control freak landlords who lived beneath us monitored how often they heard the sweeper) but that was a no-go. Hour after hour of this frustration succeeded in bringing my lovely bride to near-homicidal levels of frustration.

When I finally woke up, Missy was in NO mood to hug and kiss. She pushed me back into the bedroom and hissed, "You have GOT to get rid of him!"

"Huh? Martin?" I asked groggily. "Why?"

"Why?!" she exclaimed. "He's been asleep on the couch ALL DAY! I can't get ANYTHING done."

Knowing on which side my bread is buttered, I wisely advised, "Just go ahead and do what you need to do. He'll wake up and get the hint."

So Missy washed our dishes as noisily as possible.

Martin didn't twitch.

Missy fired up the sweeper and cleaned every inch of the wall-to-wall carpet in our two-bedroom apartment, slamming the vacuum into furniture every chance she had.

Martin didn't even snort or roll over.

We sat at our kitchen/dining room table and talked noisily.

Still nothing.

Finally, of course, right before Missy had to leave for work, Martin arose from his golden slumber. Did he apologize for inconveniencing us all day? Nope. Did he at least act sheepish and awkward? Hell no! Did this piss my wife off even more? Hell yes! Did Martin have an aha moment and get the fuck out our apartment in a timely fashion? Hahahahaha! That's HILARIOUS!

That sloth motherfucker stayed until I had to go back to work for another round of third shift. By that time I was feeling pretty cool with earning a life sentence for murdering the fat bastard. Thanks to him, NOTHING was accomplished at our home for an entire day, other than marital discord.

My reason for sharing this anecdote, and I do have a point, is that Martin was a complete hypocrite douchebag. His mouth spewed Christianese in the name-it-claim-it/fake-it-take-it dialect, but the reason the idiot was a pizza delivery boy at the ripe old age of twenty-nine was quite obvious. Here was a fine example of an entitled, lazy-assed American who thought he could dick around all night, sleep all day, work a minimum wage job, and somehow...somehow, because he prayed and had faith, fame and fortune would float down like Manna from heaven and land in his lap. In his mind, he was *clearly* a musical genius that the world must eventually recognize, worship, and support. There's *no way* people wouldn't beg to kiss his ring or shine his shoes. He was a Guitar God, for fuck's sake!

*

We ended up writing and recording two songs with Martin. One was a mid-tempo rocker ("Caught Up to Paradise") about the Rapture. Nothing about my bass line was ever criticized during the song's composition and we rehearsed the shit out of it to avoid wasting money in the studio but suddenly, once it was being recorded, I didn't know how to play, according to Martin.

After my tracking was done and the engineer played the tune back for me, I remember peeling my headphones off proudly. Any musician will tell you that it just *feels* right when you've nailed a song in the studio, so my huge grin showed how tightly my bass line had locked in with Tom's drums. After that there was nothing else to do but put my guitar away and sit in the control room, basking in my achievement while watching Martin record his tracks. Hell, I was even excited about seeing what magic our newest member could conjure on his axe. It's always a blast to watch a special musician perform, right?

But, as soon as I sat down, the Guitar Genius stopped warming up so he could lean back and say, "Ya know, you *really* should learn your scales. Everything you play is in the pentatonic scale."

I may be a self-taught musician but even a dumbass like me knows that rock n' roll came from the blues, which is entirely based on the pentatonic scale. "Um, did I play bum notes or something?" I asked, in shock that a keeper performance was being criticized.

Martin's fat face contorted into a smarmy grin. "Wellllll, no, but knowing the rest of your scales would help you play even better notes, ones that go better with the chords *I'm* playing." After that I don't remember a single thing he said because my fragile little ego was bruised and my earholes slammed shut.

When it came time to record the bass line for the second song, a ballad called "Precious Hearts" (more on this tune later), it seemed like I'd forgotten how to play my own instrument. Every time the red light came on my hands shook and my mind raced. Instead of just letting go and locking in with a tune I should be able to play in my sleep, I was defeating myself with paralysis by analysis.

Fortunately, after many stops and starts, my anger about Martin's arrogance finally kicked in. *Who the hell does this douchebag think he is? He's been in the band for a few months and already he's bashing my playing? Am I going to let this pizza boy wreck my studio experience? No way!* So, after taking a deep breath and willing my shaky hands and racing thoughts to get their shit together, I nodded to the engineer, the tape rolled, and my track was nailed in that very take.

BAM!

SUCK IT, MARTIN!

*

In retrospect, what's even more disturbing than my inability to take criticism or the Guitar God's know it all attitude are the lyrics to "Precious Hearts". If memory serves me this catchy piano ballad was mostly the brainchild of James, with an assist from Cole. While I'm sure we weren't the only songwriters to tackle the topic of child abuse, hopefully no one else addressed the issue with such glaring naiveté and stupidity.

The song describes a kid who's on the verge of snapping after being pummeled by an angry father who's told him that he's a mistake. So far so good as far as real life accuracy goes. But the second verse claims that this kid's memories become "erased" when he accepts Christ and life is now a bowl of cherries.

When I dusted off the ancient cassette of this demo to refresh my memory, these lyrics appalled me. To claim that an abused human being can have his or her traumatic memories wiped clean by the blood of the Lamb is a slap in the face to anyone who has gone through that nightmare. Modern neuroscience proves that severely negative experiences are remembered better than positive ones. Why? Because it's valuable for survival. Those humans who retained crucial memories of situations or creatures to avoid lived on to reproduce.

And my career in education has brought me face to face with kids who have to deal with the horrific repercussions of abuse on a daily basis. I've met people who were both physically beaten and sexually abused; that kind of trauma is never going to be erased.

Yes, abused children who find a healthy, supportive environment while receiving tons of therapy can mostly move on and lead happy lives. But to assert that becoming born again will stop those horrific nightmares of Daddy beating, burning, and whipping you is beyond ridiculous. To say that adults with this kind of background aren't going to have trust and relationship issues for the rest of their lives is pathetically ignorant. Granted, back then I was incredibly sheltered. My only exposure to this realm was through books and movies; none of the guys in our band had ideal childhoods, but we certainly had never benefitted from a call to Children's Services either. Finally, I'm surprised that no one called us out on this bullshit, pie-in-the-sky song after hearing us play it live. That would've been a serious wake up call for sure!

I'm not just bringing this up to critique our lyrical follies, of which there were many. The violently naïve words in this song speak to the willfully ignorant nature of Christianity's subculture. Sure, most believers know that this shit happens to kids, but how many just say they'll pray about it? When I was an avid churchgoer, almost everyone I associated with thought that getting saved was the be-all-end-all solution. Yeah, there was still work to be done to turn your life around completely, but anyone's whining about lingering psychological issues from some form of trauma was just proof that they weren't *giving it all to the Lord.* They needed to leave their troubles on Jesus' shoulders because He was able to bear the burden, not them!

To live life with such a simple, one-size-fits-all mentality is reprehensible to me now. Nothing in life is that cut and dried. Nothing is black and white. Each person is different and all of us are fighting different battles. Yes, there are universal needs and wants, but to say that religion is the panacea is ludicrous. The people who make such claims are the same folks who insist that school shootings happen because "prayer isn't allowed in school" and "God's a gentleman who won't go where He isn't wanted". Even typing that sentence makes my blood boil.

Clearly your god is made in your image if he's able to prevent child abuse or school shootings but doesn't. Obviously your god is a primitive fiction if he's such a bitchy diva that he won't intervene if his supernatural panties are in a twist about something. Anyone who sees the world through these Rose of Sharon colored glasses needs to find a personal relationship with reality! Yes, real life is messy, confusing, and dangerous, but I'd rather have the balls to face it head on instead of needing a deity to sugarcoat it. As an adult, I shouldn't need Mommy or Daddy to crush up my medicine and mix it with strawberry jam so I can choke it down.

*

After recording these tracks we ran out of money to have them properly mixed and mastered so there was no way we were sending them off to Tony Castle in this raw state, even though he said we could. You'd think we'd have taken the man up on an offer to listen to even a rough, boom box recording of the songs because this would've saved tons of money, but that would've involved common sense. Critical Dispatch was all about wasting atrocious amounts of money in order to make very little back. This habitual insistence on overkill meant we had to book some moneymaking gigs pronto. Those damn, pesky studio engineers apparently expected to be paid for their labor.

Greedy asshats!

Of course, in another example of impeccable timing, Tom confided in me that he was leaving Critical Dispatch because he felt "lead by God" to quit. So much for playing shows and finishing demos! My overall enthusiasm for the band had been waning for some time anyway but I was still bummed by this development. Virtually every band I'd ever been in had had Tom behind the kit. Great chemistry in a rhythm section isn't easy to find so losing my old high school chum depressed me to no end. But, what could I do? Who was I to argue with a direct message from God?

At our next band practice Tom revealed his news, assuring everyone that he'd prayed about it for a long time before making a move. Most of us made half-hearted attempts to convince him to pray about it a little more in case his personal feelings were distorting heaven's signal, but his mind was clearly made up.

As soon as Tom left the rehearsal space we wracked our brains about potential, established drummers who'd be able to hit the ground running instead of starting from scratch. We needed someone who learned quickly, was easy to work with, and had a stable walk with Christ. Suddenly the answer was obvious. A band that I'd filled in on bass for, Look East, had just broken up. Their drummer, Don, was a cool dude and rockin' skinbeater. Since I knew him better than anyone in our band the duty of asking him to audition was delegated to me, and I was more than happy to do it. One of the few beefs we'd all had about Tom was that he was very moody and unpredictable. Don was very even keel and happy go lucky, so the change could be a breath of fresh air.

While his tryout got off to a rough start it finished well so we asked Don to join. After praying about it he gladly accepted.

For once, replacing a member happened quickly and efficiently. We were pumped, hoping this was a sign of great things to come. Still, we held off on booking gigs to ensure that Don was at least partially integrated into the fold. At the time I had no doubt whatsoever that Critical Dispatch's rhythm section chemistry was not experiencing a setback. After all, I'd rehearsed many times and played one gig with this guy and it went so well that I briefly flirted with the idea of being in two bands at once.

Boy, was I wrong!

Inexplicably, Don had developed a problem with tempo. He was constantly speeding up and slowing down, not to mention forgetting sections of songs. Every normal drummer battles this to a certain extent, but Don's issues were so blatant that any Joe Blow in the audience would detect them. We tried to convince him to play with a metronome or click track, but he was too proud. Fortunately, though, with weeks and weeks of practice we at least sounded decent enough to book a small, test run show at a local church.

Oddly enough, my only dim memories of that gig are of our soundcheck. Instead of fond recollections of a massive audience cheering, headbanging, and singing, there are only flashes of lively, pre-show banter and chuckling to reminisce about. Maybe I'm reading too much into it but perhaps my brain chooses to focus on this is because our musical chemistry was flat lining at that point. The only thing keeping me hanging around was the brotherhood of being in a band. All in all, just like everything else in Critical Dispatch at the time, this show was very blah, forgettable, and forced. It felt like we were all treading water with no hope for rescue.

And we were right.

Chapter 35

Once I'd become thoroughly fascinated with Universalist doctrine, I quit attending the Church of God of Prophecy and began frequenting a Bible study at Jeff Priddy's home. Missy went with me a couple of times but, at that point, she was content to pursue her own spirituality from home. She was not only adjusting to a new, high-pressure job but we were also dealing with the fallout from my parents' divorce. With all of that going on, Missy was just relieved that we now had Sundays and Wednesdays free. Plus, Priddy's nitpicking, linguistic analysis form of bible study bored her to tears.

My orthodox friends (including my mom; Dad just didn't want me in a cult) would wrinkle their brows worriedly and ask, "Where are you going to church these days?" [Translation: "I suspect that you're backsliding into the fiery pits of Lucifer's Lair. What do you have to say for yourself?"]. I'd just assure them that I was currently a member of a small assembly that met in a friend's living room. This did nothing to convince them of my eternal safety but it did get them off my back for a while.

Apparently, even though the ENTIRE Christian church started with groups of the faithful coming together in each other's homes, such activity no longer constituted adequate worship or edification. When I would remind my inquisitors of this they'd reply with something like, "Well, yeah, but you really should find a *real* church. A Bible study's fine but what about praise and worship time? And how do you expect to be blessed financially if you aren't tithing?"

These questions would lead to soul searching followed by consulting with Mr. Priddy and the others at Bible study. They would share verses with me that proved believers were no longer required to live under Old Testament law. "Yes," they said. "We are expected to live righteously, but Christ's sacrifice redeems us, not handing over cash to the church or doing good deeds." This chafed against most of what I'd been taught my whole life. Sure, orthodox doctrine preaches that grace, not works, leads to salvation but it also relies heavily on the threat of punishment both during and after our lifetimes.

Hmmm, was this another inconsistency in church doctrine that my brain could no longer sweep under the carpet?

Once, I remember confiding in Jeff that I was having trouble with ogling a hot young woman in one of my college classes. "Dude," I whined. "I love my wife and would *never* cheat on her, but I keep catching myself sneaking peaks at this gorgeous chick's boobs in my lit class."

Priddy just chuckled and replied, "You're trying to live under the Law and save yourself by resisting a natural instinct.

Next time she walks by, take a good, long look at her chest and enjoy it. Once you stop straining to be perfect and punishing yourself for falling short, the urge to gawk at her hooters will go away." And, for the most part, he was right. As I retrained my brain to just relax and be human, the dog-chasing-his-own-tail behavior I'd been torturing myself with gradually melted away. For the first time in my entire life, Christianity was liberating me instead of binding me into a solipsist hell.

*

Shortly after that ho-hum drummer test run gig, I decided to throw in the towel as well. A lot of praying and mustering of courage preceded my announcement, but it had become increasingly clear that I was only sticking around out of habit and fear of change. In fact, just like the end of my membership at the Church of God of Prophecy, this time period became infused with an overwhelming urge to simplify my cluttered life. Once again, too many activities that were once done out of passion were now only motivated by guilt, and they were dominating my life. What if I died tomorrow? Would I want to be stuck in these hamster wheels, achieving nothing and feeling numb inside?

HELL NO!

Fortunately there wasn't much of a fuss about my resignation. I think everyone could sense but didn't want to face the fact that Critical Dispatch was a brain dead patient being kept alive by life support. Ever since Gill's departure our bodily systems were gradually shutting down one by one. Now it was time to face the fact that the plug needed to be pulled so, shortly after I quit, the band broke up forever. Don't get me wrong, I certainly wasn't the brains of the operation, more like the second to last organ to wink out in that comatose patient's body. So, instead of going out with a bang, C.D. gently breathed its last breath and shit the bed with little or no notice from the outside world. And, sadly, everyone still had to pitch in and make payments on the PA and RV loans, until they were sold, just like a family is left with medical bills after a loved one passes away.

Even though I knew I'd made the right decision, I still remember feeling sad about the end of an era, not to mention (pathetically) the loss of adulation from committed fans. But it also felt as if a decaying albatross had been lifted from my shoulders. Once again I could breathe as a free man, and it was good, even if I didn't know what the hell to do with myself.

Chapter 36

Being the neurotic freak that I am, my newfound inner peace didn't last long. Life has a way of waiting until things are proceeding nicely and as soon as my confidence begins to soar: BAM! A suckerpunch to the gonads doubles me over into an unbroken circuit of self-absorbed psychoses.

Case in point: at this time one of my closest friends, Luke, was diagnosed with Huntington's chorea (or Huntington's disease), which is a rare neurological disorder with symptoms similar to Parkinson's. Within eight months I watched in agony as my pal, the insanely hilarious and intelligent former Marine who was my near-constant rock concert companion, became wheelchair bound, lapsed into a coma, then died. This was on the heels of a childhood friend (a Christian in the truest sense of the word) being killed by a drunk driver and followed by my father-in-law dying from cancer.

Insomnia began to torture me for days and days on end. My eyes ached and my brain felt as if someone had encased it in concrete. While driving to college I had what I'd later figure out was my first anxiety attack. Unfortunately, many more would follow during classes, at family dinners, etc. I lived in fear of panic overtaking me and people gaping at my trembling hands. I just *knew* that they'd think I was a nutcase who needed to be locked up. Within no time I was a withdrawn basket case, avoiding social interaction like the plague. Simple daily tasks like signing my name, reading aloud, or eating in front of others became impossible.

At work I confided in a trusted Christian friend, we'll call her Brandy, who was like a sister to me, revealing my embarrassing stories with the common ingredients of gasping for air, racing heartbeat, feeling trapped, and shaking hands. Did this friend urge me to seek professional help? Nope. She said, "Well, maybe God's trying to tell you that you aren't supposed to become a teacher." Even in my frazzled state I knew this was a faulty hypothesis.

Then, in desperation after the insomnia and anxiety continued, I called my old buddy Pastor Pete, not because I trusted his advice more than anyone else's but because he'd studied to be a counselor. After I bared my soul, my former shepherd advised that, "These types of problems usually are the result of unconfessed sins. God's trying to get your attention."

Another so-called friend and former Critical Dispatch keyboard player, James, suggested, "Maybe all of this education isn't good for you. Maybe learning all of these worldly things from these professors is driving a wedge between you and God. What if He's trying to tell you that college is pulling you away from Him?" *Gee, thanks,* I wanted to say. *All of this you-should-be-beating-yourself-up-WAY-more-than-you-currently-are wisdom is just SOOOOO soothing!*

It's quite telling that no one urged me to find a shrink and get put on meds. Instead, the church's answer was to encourage me to blame myself and stop getting an education. Considering I eventually came within inches of attempting suicide, I have to wonder how many folks who've struggled with mental illness have ended up six feet under, thanks to religion. I'm not saying that Christianity is the only reason that I didn't seek proper medical help (fearing that people would think I was nuts and that medication would turn me into an uncreative zombie were also factors) but too many people base serious life decisions entirely around what their religion tells them. I was battling a life-threatening neurosis and the church's prescription was for me to beat my sinful self up *more*, confess whatever sins I was keeping secret, and stop learning stuff!

I know I've said this before but it bears repeating: Christianity is the only army that shoots its wounded.

*

Even though I was dealing with ups and downs from my anxiety disorder this was still not a totally unhappy time. Unlike many of the eighteen year-olds I was in college with, I was enjoying the fuck out of learning everything I could, with the exception of having to memorize every bone in a cat's skeleton for Biology 101.

One of my favorite classes was Philosophy. When I entered the class my faith was fairly unshakable. By the time the final exam was done my life would never be the same. Our teacher, a skinny, awkward professor, was a master at presenting material with infectious passion. First, we'd read and take notes on a famous philosopher's ideas, then he'd pose thought-provoking dilemmas that forced us to apply these theories to real life scenarios. Our class discussions were so intellectually stimulating that I could almost feel my brain being kneaded and stretched like pizza dough.

During one lesson, the prof told us a story about his father-in-law, a retired pastor. This man had never cussed and had always treated his wife like a queen. Everyone in the community loved and respected him. He was the epitome of what a good Christian man should be. Then he had a stroke. Apparently his frontal lobe was severely damaged because this once gentle man was now full of rage and aggression. He cursed like a sailor and started hitting his devoted wife. "How do we make sense of this, from a Christian point of view?" the professor asked. "This is still the same man. It was his physical body that was affected. What about his soul? If it's located in the brain, was it affected as well? Or is his good, God-fearing soul trapped within his malfunctioning brain? Will he be judged and held accountable for this on Judgment Day?"

This man's plight really made me think. How could Jesus allow this godly, loving husband to turn into such a hellish monster? Was this how a creator should treat a loyal worshipper?

We also studied concepts such as free will. All of us thought the notion of humans not having free will was ludicrous, at first. But, after studying the thoughts of philosophy's heavyweights, any of us with remotely open minds had to admit that we are, to a very large extent, slaves to nature and nurture.

This lesson prepared me for Jeff Priddy's Bible study in which he proved that scripture doesn't (clearly) assert that people have free will either. There are plenty of verses swaying back and forth on this issue (you can dig into that yourself, if you're interested) but the number of scriptures implying that all has been decided beforehand far outnumber the others. So Priddy's Bible study prompted me to ask what kind of demented deity would predetermine that even one person would end up simmering in his own juices for eternity? This, he posited, also lent credence to universalism's belief that everyone would eventually be saved. Many might have to be purified *for a season* in flames but God wasn't a complete douche because He'd eventually let them out to frolic around His new kingdom in the second earthly paradise, whatever the fuck that means.

Between my brain being twisted and stretched in Philosophy and then Bible study at Jeff's house, my gray matter was learning to flex its muscles again. Questioning everything was again part of my daily routine. Just because someone was a supposed authority figure didn't mean that what they said was gospel, including Mr. Priddy. After a while it started to seem like he was doing an awful lot of gymnastic contortions and flips to make the Bible stop contradicting itself. "Well, yes, it does say that we're going to burn in Hell forever if we don't accept God, but that's just a poor translation. Okay, the Word does state in one part that good folks go to heaven after they die and in another part it describes a New Jerusalem, but that's fine because it's really all just blah, blah, blah. Yes, it says we'll be judged for our actions while also telling us that we have no free will, but blah, blah, blah, blah, blah." All of these manic attempts to rationalize the patchwork nature of the Bible did nothing but slowly convince me that it was just a massive quilt of human superstitions, poorly stitched together over the centuries by a large number of people.

*

One day, while driving home from Bible study at the Priddy residence, a thought popped into my head: *Hmm...we're all going to be saved eventually and there is no Hell. I believe that now. This is the first step back to atheism.*

THWAP! My head jerked back against my car's seat.

NO! I shouted inside my head. *No way. I'm not going to be an atheist again!*

This is the first step back to atheism.

NO!

It was as if I was desperately trying to slam a mental door to keep that stray thought from ever rearing its ugly head again. But it didn't work. The more I tried to suppress it that day, and from then on, the more it resurfaced.

This is the first step back to atheism.

*

For a long time I suppressed the thought of returning to godlessness. I continued attending Bible study at Jeff Priddy's house whenever I could but found myself feeling less and less motivated to go. Of course, when I stayed home my church-i-fried conscience berated me with statements such as: *See, once you got rid of the fear of Hell and replaced it with universal salvation, this is what happened! Now you're too lazy to study God's word or even attend an informal Bible study. That's how you show your devotion to Jesus after He was crucified for your sins?*

What if all your orthodox friends are right? What if you ARE going to burn forever?

Then my newly liberated, rational brain would storm in to my defense: *This is probably just a phase. You've swung from one end of the Christian spectrum to the other. Of course you'll go through a transition period of apathy. After a while your desire for scripture study will return. The more you chastise yourself the more you feed the legalistic urge to try to earn your salvation. Besides, why would God roast you forever in Hell for believing He has the power to save everyone and doesn't want to damn most people? That's insane!*

At first this went on and on, round and round in my brainpan pretty much nonstop but it gradually diminished in frequency. Being an incredibly busy undergraduate student while working full time in a grocery store certainly helped alleviate the solipsism. After all, a decadent quantity of sleep during this period was about five hours. There were semesters that required me to read twenty novels for literature classes, along with education textbook chapters, creating projects over those chapters, writing lesson and unit plans to use after graduation, and composing papers of every shape and size. It's hard for even *my* neurotic brain to fixate on religious self-torture when it's completely absorbed with enduring such an inhuman workload.

*

One book that I was assigned during this hectic period, *The Epic of Gilgamesh*, made a huge impact as well. If you haven't heard of this ancient myth, it's a flood story from Mesopotamia. While reading it I didn't know that many believe the Bible borrowed from this epic poem, but my copy of the paperback quickly became full of underlined passages and notes about the similarities. The hero of the flood story may have been named Utnapishtim, but he was told (by a god) to build a boat (with exact dimensions), then load up his family and the animals, all in order to survive a storm that lasted six days and nights. Then his craft crash-lands on a mountain. Sound familiar? Oh, and he sends out three birds to see if the coast is clear: a raven, swallow, and dove. Apparently the authors of the Bible chose to let the first two birds hit the editing room floor in order to stick with the Judeo-Christian dove motif.

The Epic of Gilgamesh both fascinated and infuriated me. I've always loved folklore so the story rekindled a neglected passion for mythology, but it also opened my eyes to the plagiarism of my culture's so-called holy book. If the epic story of Noah was lifted from a Sumerian poem, what else from the Bible was ripped off? And why was I just finding out about this bullshit NOW?

My anger over this spurred me to delve back into global folklore to search for other plagiarized source materials. Of course I found creation, redemption, salvation, and apocalypse myths from a myriad of different cultures. Most origin tales featured order being created from watery chaos, which some experts trace back to mothers going through childbirth. Pretty much all homo sapien tribes had one of their kin who fucked up big time, which made it necessary to get back on the good side of their god or gods. Still, even after finding forgiveness for our wretchedness, we always seemed to screw up again so most civilizations could only look forward to enduring a devastatingly cataclysmic battle between good and evil.

And yet, a funny thing happened as these universal motifs revealed themselves one by one: my intense anger toward religion dimmed to a much duller roar. Instead of staying perched on my high horse of judgment I began to feel empathy. How could there NOT be countless similarities in our mythologies? When those stories were concocted, weren't we all just primitive humans desperately trying to make sense of existence? It's not like we had any textbooks or manuals to give us a leg up, so we had to verbalize our own explanations for reality around campfires and in caves, revising and embellishing them over the centuries. As civilizations traded and mingled, myths latched on to departing travelers like bacteria seeking more fertile hosts in which to multiply and mutate.

Unfortunately for these primitive stories, the printing press was invented, improved and popularized. Ancient, germ-like tales became preserved like flies in amber, which wasn't problematic until science revised and increased the world's collective wisdom, revealing the quaintness of yesterday's wisdom.

Am I saying that there are no timeless truths in folklore? Absolutely not! Can you name at least ten people who could improve their character by spending some quality time with the likes of Athena, Thor, Arthur, or Isis? I know I can without even breaking a sweat. These heroes and heroines encapsulate desirable human values both then and now, which is exactly why they fascinate us to this day. Almost all of the best characters from ancient (and modern) stories demonstrate key traits that have helped our species thrive: courage, resourcefulness, dignity, kindness, etc.

Plus, all of them are quite flawed; if they weren't how could we relate? And I'm not just referring to the human heroes from mythology. Look at the gods we've worshipped. Zeus was a temperamental man-whore. Isis had a bit of a necrophilia problem. Yahweh was constantly getting green with envy. Now, I hear a lot of atheists snorting with condescension about the glaringly manmade personalities of our deities but, again, it would be impossible for the fruit of our (primitive or modern) brains to be truly transcendent. Yes, the horniness and insecurity of the gods illuminate their human origins, but that's no reason to get all snooty toward them. After all, they're just representations of the hopes, dreams, and faults of humanity.

Show some respect for your elders, you pricks!

Chapter 37

As it turns out, my phase of disinterest in Bible study (and all things churchy) never ended. For months and months my heart and mind grew apart from religion's trappings. Before I knew it I'd once again become an atheist, which I (again) quietly accepted.

Neither Missy nor I remember any specifics of my coming out of the atheist closet to her. My lovely bride, however, does recall that we had a lot of family drama and tons of stress (over gearing up to move because I was interviewing for teaching jobs) and all she could think was, *Seriously, with everything going on right now THAT is what occupies your brain?!* Apparently this earth-shattering revelation of a massive change in my worldview was an annoyance in the face of life's practical concerns.

Who knew?

None of my associates from the smorgasbord of churches I'd attended knew for sure where I stood and there was no way in hell they'd hear it from *my* mouth. I'd spent six years spewing Christian propaganda in all directions so my newly re-found lack of faith was actually quite humbling. How could I go around being a smug, outspoken non-believer while these friends and family members had just seen me making a fool out of myself for Jesus? And why in the world would I boast loudly and proudly that I'd just escaped a religious pyramid scheme that robbed me of common sense, the chance to sow my wild oats during my early twenties, and ten percent of my already pathetic wages?

Since Willard is such a tiny town, everyone assumed that my Bible-thumping identity was set in stone. In fact, they probably still presume that to this day. But during this two-year period of clandestine disbelief I had to *constantly* ward off questions about my current church affiliation and spiritual status with politely vague reassurances. Virtually all of the holy inquisitors responded with sad, pained smiles and invitations to attend their churches. Their lips were saying, "Okay, Stephen. I'm glad you're doing alright. You're welcome at our church anytime!" but every bit of their body language and tone of voice communicated a different message: "Well, it's *quite* obvious you've backslidden, brother. My heart aches for you. Life will always be meaningless unless you see the world *exactly* as I do!"

Other than the hours I spent in my college classes, there was no escape from these awkward conversations or, even worse, the believers who outright browbeat me with undisguised, condemning sermons. By the time I finally earned my bachelors degree and first teaching license, the constant harassment from my former peers eroded pretty much every ounce of empathy that folklore study had restored for organized religion. It was hard, if not impossible, to feel anything but hatred after being used as my former church friends' whipping boy for two long years.

Sadly, most Christians have no idea that *the church* has created many of the angry, militant atheists who are out there picketing, petitioning and suing to remove God's name and influence from our culture. Aside from a few know-it-all douchebags in the world, most people are willing to live and let live. Even though I'm not a secular uber-activist, I *was* willing to lead a perfectly silent, secular existence until the Soldiers of Jesus Christ kept shoving their beliefs down my throat.

Who doesn't get tired of being told they're worthless and unworthy of love? What rational human being can tolerate hearing that there's only ONE way to live life and all who deviate from it will suffer the flames of Hell? There wasn't one single, solitary time that I tried to de-convert *any* of these people, so why the fuck did they have the right to corner *me* like a dirty, diseased animal?

*

Fortunately for the Blossom City's citizens, my first teaching job required my heathen ass to relocate over one

301

hundred miles away. This move wasn't only good for them; in fact, it's easily one of the best things that's ever happened to Mr. and Mrs. Hines. We may have been terrified about moving three hours away from everyone and anything we'd ever known, but we were also ecstatic about wiping our slate clean. There wasn't a soul in southern Ohio who expected us to be devout Christians. Nobody knew that I'd had long hair and played bass in Critical Dispatch. No one gave a rat's ass about my past, only my future.

*

Of course, I'd be a boldfaced liar if I claimed that our move to the opposite side of the Buckeye state was without incident. My beautiful, resourceful bride adapted quite easily, coming as she does from a family that was rather nomadic when she was a child. I, however, came from a long line of mental health consumers and was still in denial about seeking help for my anxiety disorder.

In case you don't know, people with mental illnesses have a much harder time adjusting to big changes. We need routine, and relocating to begin a new career obliterated every bit of that for me. For twenty-eight years I'd lived in the same little town. The only job I'd ever had was now gone, and it was unbelievably jarring to suddenly come to the realization that, no matter where I went, there wasn't a single, familiar face to be found.

At first I was so busy being a first year teacher that all of the change was mostly refreshing, yet still frustratingly disorienting. It was only during the short snippets of downtime in my schedule that my illness caught up with me, allowing depression and anxiety to consume me. While the phobias I'd developed (eating and writing in front of others) from past panic attacks were still restricting my daily activities, I was still maintaining a normal lifestyle.

And then came winter.

*

My first Christmas Break as a teacher began as a joyous occasion. Yes, I still had papers to grade but at least there was time to sleep in, visit family, and recharge my batteries. The problem with that, other than the obvious disruption to my new routine, was that family gatherings for holidays revolve around eating in front of others. Until my anxiety disorder surfaced I'd never appreciated how many human interactions involve meals. If you meet a new friend, they either want to meet for a meal or have you come over for one. When you start a new job your coworkers want to take you out to lunch. A religious holiday needs to be celebrated? Strap on the feedbag, dude!

Needless to say, our entire time back home was, for me, full of humiliating failures that caused my symptoms to snowball at an alarming rate. If I had an opportunity to slink away from the table with my plate then I did. If not, a full-blown panic attack would force me to either claim I was full or not feeling well. Yes, I'd been having problems in our new town, but I'd successfully avoided dwelling on them by staying busy. With four family gatherings providing ample opportunity for anxiety-ridden torture and plenty of time to dwell upon my crumbling ability to socialize, I returned from our road trip a broken man.

All I need to do is get through the second week of break, then get back in the groove at work, I thought. *My symptoms will calm down because there won't be time to fixate on them. Sure, things will still be awkward but I can make it work.*

But Old Man Winter had other plans.

*

At the very end of my vacation, our area was hit with a massive snowstorm. Christmas Break was extended first with one snow day, then another, and another. By the time the White Death was done paralyzing civilization we'd used ten consecutive snow days. Today, that much time off would be cause for a celebration involving me running around the neighborhood wearing nothing but a white thong and huge smile. Back then it just provided more and more time to dwell on my humiliating mental illness. Every waking moment became full of crippling anxiety, followed by all-consuming depression. Now that I'd finally achieved my dream of becoming a teacher here I was going batshit crazy.

What if I couldn't get my act together? What if I tried to teach and had a panic attack? There's no way my students would respect me if my hands shook so badly that I couldn't even write on the board for them.

By the time school was finally back in session, I managed to scrape through one in-service day and normal round of classes with students before hitting the wall. Every second of those two days took a Herculean effort to grind through. My muscles were so tight that my skull felt on the verge of caving in. I had no appetite. Sleep was impossible. Obviously I needed help IMMEDIATELY.

*

At first I tried hypnotherapy. In college I'd read about people using hypnosis to take the mind-over-matter concept to new heights. Patients had overcome addictions and phobias by tapping into the nearly limitless potential of the human brain, so why couldn't I?

So I began seeing a very nice, middle-aged lesbian lady, we'll call her Dr. Cameron, twice a week. She not only counseled and hypnotized me in her office, but she also supplied self-hypnosis tapes to listen to every night. At first this treatment seemed to help but it soon became clear that the power of the trance was no match for the might of my neurosis. When I told my hypnotherapist about my continuing struggles, she asked if I had a higher power. I hung my head and said, fully expecting heaping amounts of judgment and animosity, "No, I'm an atheist."

"Well, lots of people with your disorder find comfort and strength through a belief in God. Do you think you could try to believe and see if it helps?"

I sat and thought about it for a few minutes, trying to will myself back to my former state. Here I was, a nervous, tattered wreck, desperate for any lifeline to help hold things together, on the verge of hospitalization, fearing all of the humiliation that would certainly come when everyone in my new community found out, but I just couldn't find a single ounce of motivation to believe again.

"No," I sighed, shaking my head. "I've been down that road before. Trust me, I've tried praying for help with this but it just feels hollow, like I'm faking it out of desperation."

Dr. Cameron smiled, her eyes full of concern, sympathy and compassion. "Maybe you should give it anther shot, then."

Out of respect for her heartfelt faith in a higher power, I agreed to give belief another try.

Cut to me, in the full grip of a panic attack, huddled in our small apartment's bathroom, gasping for breath, a couple nights later. Hiding from everyone, including my wife, at least allowed me to freak out unobserved. *Come on, Stephen,* I thought. *Maybe it'll help. Anything's better than this! You're coming unglued. Do you want to lose your job after five grueling years in college? What do you have to lose?*

My heart was racing. Cold, fiery electric arcs shot through my limbs. It was almost impossible to hold any coherent thought pattern. Still, desperate times call for desperate measures, so I mustered every bit of willpower I could spare and tried to shoehorn the savior back into my brain.

Jesus, if you're there, I prayed. *Please keep me from losing my mind!*

Instead of any comforting touch from the Prince of Peace, I felt like a pathetic fraud, whimpering pleas for help into a cold, dark vacuum. Still, maybe if I tried harder to believe He would help me.

Between racing, terrified thoughts I tried again.

God, if you're there you know I don't believe but I will gladly follow you till my dying day if you make yourself known to me now. My eyes squeezed closed and I held myself while rocking back and forth. *All I need is a few minutes with peace of mind. That's all. Just something to get me through. PLEASE?!*

Again, I felt and heard nothing.

Absolutely nothing.

Nothing was all that was out there to receive my intercession.

Being on the verge of suicide, pleading for help from a higher power, and receiving ZERO comfort or aid was the last nail in Yahweh's coffin. Yes, I was pretty dead set in my unbelief before this, but if God gave a shit whether I lived or died couldn't He have at least lifted an incorporeal finger? All He had to do was give me a minute or two of peace and calm. That would've gotten me through at least another couple days. Then He could've thrown me another bone, stringing me along back to mental health. What a golden opportunity to seal the deal for my eternal soul! Yet He couldn't be bothered to do jack shit.

Of course there will be readers saying that God doesn't jump through hoops to gain believers. Why should He perform any more signs and wonders to prove He exists? Hasn't He done enough? Or they'll claim He allowed me to go through this in the hopes that I'd rededicate my life to Him. Or He's omniscient and knew that I wouldn't go through with suicide. Well, if all of that's true then He's a heartless, lazy dickhead who gets off on watching His creation suffer. I wouldn't wish panic attacks and depression on my worst enemy! And, if God's all knowing then

He certainly must have seen that I still think He is a manmade fiction today. So we're back to the old conundrum: If God's omnipotent and doesn't intervene, then He's evil. If Yahweh's omniscient and knows His trials and tests won't bring someone to salvation, then He's a sociopathic fiend who enjoys torturing His toys in both this life and the great beyond.

After this last ditch attempt at belief (which occurred during a forty-eight hour panic attack that almost ended with me stepping in front of a huge truck) I finally sought professional help. And so, inch by inch, I clawed and scratched my way back up from the cliff's edge with bloody, cracked fingernails, slowly regaining control of my life, with assistance from medicine (invented by scientists) and therapy (developed by experts who used scientific methods), of course.

And, even with life's ups and downs, I'm happier than ever.

NO thanks to God!

Chapter 38

Although I had already flirted with giving in to the anger I felt toward organized religion, my fight for sanity effectively put that phase on pause. So, once my mental health stabilized, my repressed atheist angst slowly bubbled back up to the surface. Still, my militant atheist stage didn't really become obvious to anyone outside my household until years later.

For a while I was content to just make snarky comments to my wife, or other likeminded friends, about any Christian hypocrisy or inanity that I observed. For example, during this period I wrote and recorded a metal song in my tiny, basement studio. I had all of the drum, bass, and guitar tracks finished but there were no lyrics. As I always do, I leafed through my bedside journal full of story and song ideas and stumbled upon an angry (and, in retrospect, not-so original or well-written) atheist rant that I'd scribbled down. It was a perfect fit for the music.

So, one beautiful Saturday morning, just before the Buckeyes' football game was due to start, I hurriedly set up a microphone. I was in a good mood when I started recording but, with each line that was spoken, years and years of repressed anger added greater intensity, reaching a powerful climax at the end and resulting in a cathartic sigh of relief, which I kept in the song.

When I came up from the basement, Missy was staring at me, wide-eyed with concern. "Are you alright?" she asked.

"Yeah," I said, baffled by her concern. "Why wouldn't I be?"

"Well, whatever you just recorded down there sounded pretty intense."

Smiling while turning on the OSU game, I nonchalantly replied, "Ah, it was just a song."

Here, for your edification, are that song's lyrics:

Recipe for a Holy Vessel

(https://soundcloud.com/stephenhines/11-recipeforaholyvessel)

Say a little prayer

To a god who doesn't exist

When He doesn't answer

You can't get pissed

It just wasn't His will

He knows what's best

And all this pain you feel

It's all just a test

Deny your animal instincts

They are sinful and wrong

Pray to be delivered from them

And sing a holy song

Avoid questioning God's word

For that is unholy heresy

You must accept its contradictions

(And ill-logic) deaf and blindly

Sautee 180 pounds of human primate superstition

Stir it up with an unhealthy dose of guilt

Add a couple dashes of self-righteousness, egocentrism, and

homophobia

Sprinkle in some misogyny, dogmatism, and ignorance

Bake at 777 degrees until the mixture becomes a blackened,

hard, heart-shaped mass

Hollow it out in the center and fill with holy water blessed by a

pedophile priest

Don't ever forget

That He's always watching

Your every transgression

Instantly judging

Divine entrapment

As you take the bait

Indulging your flesh

And sealing your fate

Stop begging forgiveness

You'll never measure up

Your pathetic attempts

Only add sorrow to your cup

For He is a jealous god

Living through you

Too holy to ever sin

Yours gets Him through!

*

And so, given the fact that my music has approximately two rabid fans, the proverbial cat of my militant atheism was still safely in the bag. But then I was foolish enough to accept a Facebook friend request from my old friend James, the former keyboard player of Critical Dispatch.

Initially this social networking experiment went well. We talked about our families, careers, the Critical Dispatch days, joking back and forth about rocking out, wearing ridiculous stage clothes, and other assorted hijinx that only former bandmates could have bonded over. Eventually, though, my former guru's true colors just *had* to manifest when I shared a pro-atheist meme. James immediately leapt into the fray with this tried and true apologetics nugget of wisdom: "If you don't believe in God then how do you know right from wrong? The Ten Commandments and Jesus' Sermon on the Mount are the basis for our constitution and laws, man."

After much thought I replied, "Right and wrong are mostly universal concepts, regardless of culture or religion. Even our pet cats understand basic concepts like fairness, self-defense, and love. They can't read so it must be something basic that's necessary to survival as a species. Besides, if you're only doing the right thing out of fear of damnation then are you even really a good person?"

There was no counterargument, only a different question: "Well, then, without God how can your life have any meaning or purpose? If you're not living for Him, what's the point?"

"My purpose is just to become the best person I can be by being a good husband, friend, and citizen. I'm a teacher! What could be nobler than perpetuating a love of learning? And, as a writer, if I can help someone escape a stressful day by entertaining them, making them laugh, or providing a new perspective (hopefully all of those) then what could be better?" I counter-sermonized.

"But," James retorted. "Without God you still can't get into heaven by doing these things."

"I'm not trying to score points for the afterlife. I'm just trying to be an ethical human being." This quieted him down for a while. I'm not the best debater but James was used to being able to overpower people who were already on the cusp of converting but hadn't made the leap and that didn't apply to this scenario.

Later I shared a news article about evolution, which, of course, brought James back out of the woodwork with this gem: "You mean to tell me that everything came about by accident? Random chance just happened to create everything?"

Sigh. "No, but that's a common misconception. Evolution isn't necessarily a theory that claims all the right things just randomly came together to create people or birds, etc. Evolution just states that nature, through trial and error, is gradually adapting to change." Yeah, I know that's not the greatest explanation, but give me a break: I'm an English major!

James returned to neutral-only comments, but my old friend has never been one to miss a chance to (in his mind) establish his dominance. In no time flat he was pouncing on almost everything I said in the social networking realm, including a very emotional topic: a former student's suicide. James knew only one or two surface facts about the situation through my grief-stricken post about the issue, but that didn't stop him from blasting me with fire and brimstone. True to form, he seized some imaginary, moral high ground and began hurling stones of judgment at my head. But, unlike the Stephen of yesteryear, I was now a confident, self-sufficient man who wasn't about to stand for this self-righteous bullshit. After reminding

315

him that he was indeed a holier-than-thou dick, I unfriended him and deleted everything he'd ever posted on my Facebook wall.

The main sticking point for me in this situation is the (sadly) typical Christian response to a human dilemma: "When a similar situation happened to me, then this is how it was handled. Therefore, everyone else must deal with what appears to be parallel problems, based on the dearth of facts I possess, in exactly the same manner. Life is one-size-fits-all!"

Having such a simplistic, black and white outlook on life is *so* incredibly galling to me! Life is VERY complicated. There are *at least* thousands of different factors at play for each different person's dilemma. What kind of a simpleton immediately assumes that he knows EXACTLY what another completely different being should do? How narcissistic do you have to be to spew your nimrod, unsolicited opinion about what's best for someone else at them? And how stupid could a person be to do this and then be completely blindsided by the animosity that boomerangs back at them?

*

These incidents, along with a few other online mishaps, pissed me off, which lead to a different flavor of poor decision-making in the social networking realm. I began sharing angry, anti-Christian memes and articles constantly. There were sarcastic status updates urging people to keep the Thor in Thursday, not to mention a list of the top ten reasons why beer is better than God. At first my friends and family just let me blow off steam, probably shaking their heads and saying, "That Stephen. He's a hothead. Let him get this out of his system." But then my wife would see something I shared and cringe, asking if I was going to get in trouble with my employer for it. At that point, being in no mood to be told to lie low and bite my tongue, I'd snap, "Fuck 'em! These Christians always think it's okay to shove their beliefs down *my* throat. They don't have to hide who they are! Why can't I be proud of who *I* am?" It was time to fire back and even take preemptive strikes occasionally.

*

Then a coworker attempted to convert me via e-mail. My response, even though I was more than fed up with zealots (well-meaning or not), was diplomatic: "Dude, I'd never try to change your beliefs and I expect the same respect in return."

Eventually my endurance was tested even further when another coworker bought Dinesh D'Souza's *What's So Great About Christianity?* and delivered it to my classroom, claiming that, if nothing else, maybe the book would give me ammo to argue my side. Yeah, right! THAT'S why you gave me this steaming apologetics turd! I politely accepted the "gift" but there was no way in hell I'd waste time reading it. Yeah, that probably makes me a bit of a hypocrite but I read at glacier-like speeds and life is short. So, instead, I gave it to an atheist coworker as a sort of white elephant present.

The next trial of Job came out of nowhere and involved the book-bearing coworker's wife trying to debate me via e-mail. At most I'd probably said two or three sentences to this woman, yet she randomly felt "moved" to proselytize. And her oh-so original technique? She sprung Pascal's Wager on me, which basically states, *There is no way I can completely prove that there is or isn't a God. However, if there is no God and I believe in Him for my whole life, what have I lost? If there is a God and I don't believe in Him then I risk going to Hell for eternity.* My response? "This smacks of intellectual cowardice. He's basically saying he's going to hedge his bets because he's too much of a wimp to pick a side. Like an omniscient deity wouldn't know I was only paying lip service to belief to save my own ass?" Her cyber evangelism was promptly abandoned but she did succeed at making me even more irritated and fed up with Christians.

*

Shortly after that lovely exchange, a student's hyper-religious parent challenged a short story that I used in class. Apparently this modern story ("Bad Things" by Libba Bray) was just disturbing the buhjeezus out of her little seventeen year-old cherub, even though it was no worse than any classic Edgar Allen Poe tale. Did Mom call or e-mail me to discuss it, since I was the teacher who chose the literature in question? NOPE! That would be treating me like a trained professional! Did she contact my immediate supervisor to inquire? NOPE! That would be underreacting! She went all the way to the superintendent, who passed the buck back down to the assistant superintendent, who then plopped it into the curriculum director's lap.

Fortunately the suits (for once) had common sense and just asked me to reiterate my *well-documented* policy (If you don't like a story I use, call me and I'll GLADLY supply a substitute!) to the lady. Of course, when I did e-mail Mommy Dearest, she had never read my classroom rules. SHOCKER! And, even though I promised to provide an alternate story, this lady typed up several lengthy e-mail sermons about how I was leading innocent children down the fiery cobblestone path to Hell. Being the epitome of professionalism that I am, I resisted the urge to argue or tell her to get a life and/or a battery operated boyfriend.

*

To reward myself for exercising such heroic restraint with Mommy Dearest, I bought some Darwin fish stickers and an

Atheist On Board sign for my car. Just putting them in my car's windows made me jittery (I do teach in OHIO, after all) but I was sick of being forced to hide my identity and why not cheer myself up after a stressful situation? Plus I wanted to help erode the stigma that's associated with atheism. My motive wasn't to antagonize; it was to reassure. I wanted others who are unbelievers to say, "Wow! I'm not alone! Being an unbeliever doesn't make me a horrible person. There's no reason to be ashamed."

Of course, the first person to react to the Atheist On Board sign did NOT interpret the message in the way it was intended. After arriving at work one morning, I parked and proceeded to haul several heavy boxes of teaching materials toward the building's side entrance. A coworker, we'll call her Beatrice, was ahead of me and had already used her ID card to unlock the door. As she propped it open, she swiveled to look at me and half-shouted, "I don't know if I should hold the door for an ATHEIST." In the words of Taylor Mali, slam poet extraordinaire, "I bit my tongue, instead of [hers]" and lugged my boxes into the school. But Beatrice wasn't done. In the hallway her apple-red cheeks and rising tone gave away her righteous indignation. "You actually paid MONEY for that? They actually MAKE signs like that?"

"Yes," I sighed. "I bought it online."

"Well!" she huffed, acting like a cranky senior citizen instead of the forty-something woman she was. "I can't believe someone would actually pay good money for such a thing. Is that really something to be proud of?!"

At this point I'd had enough so I halted, glared at her and growled, "Ya know what, Beatrice, the sign says ATHEIST, not RAPIST. Deal with it!"

My beloved coworker could only gape as I stormed off to start my day. Of course, the perfect retort that I SHOULD have used popped into my head later. What I SHOULD have reminded Beatrice about was the infamous Two-Timing Teacher Incident from the previous school year.

You see, not too long before Beatrice basically accused me of being a turd-sucking lowlife, a teacher from our school was arrested for public sexual frolicking with an underage student. Obviously, any male educator who'd be immoral enough to get naked with a seventeen year-old girl in a parked car just had to be a godless heathen, right?

WRONG!

This guy was an outspoken, Bible thumpin' family man with a whole slew of children who'd been conceived in holy wedlock. He went to church at least three times a week and made sure everyone knew about it.

I'm guessing God wasn't his copilot on that snowy December evening while he was boning a teenage girl.

Being the upstanding citizen that I am, I didn't storm down to Beatrice's office to remind her that I've been faithfully married to the same woman for over twenty years and none of my students have *ever* been considered potential sexual conquests. Apparently my supposed rudderless, amoral lifestyle isn't THAT bad after all!

Put THAT in your hymnal and sing it loud and proud, Beatrice!

*

Within days of my confrontation with Beatrice another coworker, we'll call her Lee, stormed down to my classroom early one morning. It was before first period and I'd just finished saying good morning to several mostly unconscious teens who were shuffling through my doorway when Lee stomped up beside me. I'd been so focused on welcoming my kids that her sudden arrival startled me and I jumped a little. "Hey, Lee, what's up?"

"So," she snarled, hands on hips and looking ready for a fistfight. "I think *I* should get a sign for the other side of your car that says 'God doesn't believe in *atheists*'!"

First of all, I was NOT awake enough for a full-fledged religious debate. Secondly, this was a public school hallway and I'm a firm believer in the separation of church and state. Thirdly,

Lee's reaction to the tiny, plastic sign in my car window was the very definition of unprofessional. If teachers expect students to handle conflicts without screaming in each other's faces then we damn well better model that behavior, right? So I simply crossed my arms across my chest, clamped my big mouth closed, and gave Lee the best smile I could manage.

She huffed and puffed again, shifting her weight to the opposite hip. "What do you think about that, huh? If I get you that sign would you put it on the other side? Balance out your *little* sign's message?"

Quietly, I stayed my smiley course, refusing to take the bait.

Lee appeared on the verge of spontaneous combustion. Apparently this was NOT how the little triumphant victory for Jesus had played out in her head. This uppity Hines guy was supposed to defend himself, thus opening the floodgates for her to shower me with godly enlightenment. Why wasn't I weeping and saying the salvation prayer in the hallway while she reached up to fistbump Jehovah's phantom knuckles?!

Fortunately, in the goofy, grinning face of my pacifism, Lee couldn't maintain the level of steam necessary for continuously apoplectic anger. Her cheeks' redness slowly drained, her eyes de-bugged, and finally her feet made a valiant show of angrily stomping back to her lair.

*

The third person to give me shit over the Atheist on Board sign was my very own mother who, along with her boyfriend, came down for a visit not too long after the Lee Incident. Once greetings had been exchanged and luggage hauled into the house, everyone decided to pile into my car to head out for dinner. It ended up being guys in the front and ladies in the back and guess who picked the backseat on the driver's side?

Yep, you guessed it: Mom.

As soon as everyone was on board and I'd started the car the awkwardness was palpable. Clearing her throat, Mom growled, "So, just who IS the atheist who's on board this car?"

Fear lanced through my guts but I did my best to maintain a stoic poker face. "That would be me, Mom."

"Hmmm," she replied. "You know who *else* was an atheist? Your grandfather."

Of course, she was referring to my dad's father, a man who was known for his explosive temper and abusive corporal punishment techniques. Clearly my mother was bringing this up in an attempt to shame me via association. "What? Grandpa was an atheist?" This was news to me! I vaguely remembered him giving Granny crap over attending mass but that was it. And, although his stances on everything were very hardline throughout most of his life, old age mellowed him quite a bit.

He'd even told me how proud he was that I'd become an English teacher, which was shocking coming from a man who once punished my father for reading instead of "doing something useful."

"He sure WAS!"

Just like the confrontation with Lee, I knew this was an invitation to a fight but, again, I bit my tongue and didn't take the bait. For the rest of her visit (and ever since) the topic has never come back up, and I'm grateful. If this had happened when I was a teenager (or in my early twenties) then I'm sure a veritable Jerry Springer episode would have erupted. There's no doubt that my mother probably wishes that I was still a believer, and a Catholic one to boot, but she seems to have come to grips with it. We even recently had a very calm, amiable phone discussion about what led me to become an atheist.

Mom's more relaxed stance on religion is, in part, due to the vile treatment she received after getting divorced from my father. Even though she didn't file for or want the divorce, the church informed her that she could no longer partake in the sacraments. Never mind the fact that she'd been a loyal, mass-attending Catholic since birth. Divorce made her, in their cold, corporate eyes, a pariah. And, even though I'm an atheist, I could empathize when she shared how much this hurt her.

The other reason my atheism doesn't fire her up is just that, as far as I can gather, Mom realizes that I'm a good person and a loving son. Changing my mind on religion has done nothing to alter that. In fact, my lack of belief has led me to pursue closer relationships with loved ones and focus on how short life is.

Ironically enough, my dad (of all people) is more upset by my unbelief these days. He's always been a deist who avoids organized religion so it seems odd that my atheism rubs him the wrong way. He's never confronted me over it but he's dropped hints. How did I respond to these intimations of concern? I just promised that I'd never attempt to change his mind, unlike when I preached at him incessantly in my Christian days, and he thanked me for that.

*

As for Lee, she left me alone for a couple years. But, she later entered my classroom in a completely different way: at the end of the day and with polite, almost embarrassed humility. Instead of storming in with both guns blazing, she stumbled over her words nervously while I gaped in bewilderment. "Stephen, I know you aren't a believer—and I hope you don't get mad at me for saying this—please, don't get mad—but I just feel compelled to share something with you. Is that okay?" She looked like a dog who'd crapped on the carpet and fully expected to get hit.

"Um...yeah, Lee," I stammered. "Go ahead. I won't get mad."

She sighed in relief. "Okay, well, I just felt lead---like God wanted me to tell you that—that you have a Heavenly Father who loves you, even if you don't believe in Him."

What do you say to that? Being an eloquent wordsmith, I dropped this linguistic masterpiece on her: "Um...okay."

Lee immediately reverted to apologetic mode. "Are you sure you're not mad? Please don't get upset with me. I just felt lead to share that with you."

"I'm not mad, Lee. Really. You're fine."

"Are you sure?"

"Yeah."

"Okay, I'd better go then." She practically sprinted out of my doorway.

"Bye!" I called after her.

From the other end of the hallway I could hear her pause, then shout, "Don't be mad!" and she continued on her manic way.

*

The cumulative effect of these (and many other) interactions has created a more mature, patient, and humble Stephen Hines. I've learned to take the high road whenever it's possible. There's *no way* believers are going to be receptive to anything I say in the heat of the moment, even if I happened to be interested in changing their minds, which I'm not. I've learned that angry people aren't physiologically capable of rational thought anyway. Science tells us that the primitive, fight or flight portion of the brain is in control at times like this. Any attempt to reason with someone in this state is as pointless as teaching orderly evacuation procedures to stampeding cattle. "Now, now, Bessie! Stop sprinting into your peers! You know you're supposed to exit the corral calmly and in single file!"

Do I always manage to keep my cool? Absolutely not! But I've come a long, long way in this department. I still suck at controlling my outrage at racists and homophobes, but that's another story.

Besides, not all of my friends and acquaintances are combative. I have several pals who can ask questions and state their beliefs in a very respectful manner. We can have deep, philosophical discussions that go on for hours without a hint of anger in our minds or voices. These are the people I choose to spend my precious time with. They don't *have* to see the world the same way I do. In fact, I prefer to be surrounded by diversity. If I only talked to fellow atheists my life would be nothing but one self-congratulatory circle jerk of preaching to the choir.

FUCK THAT!

Opposing viewpoints should come together to advance our thinking, not stonewall it. There's always a time and place to agree to disagree, but why can't we help each other grow and evolve? If we're never challenged then this will never happen.

Besides, seeing the world through another person's eyes shouldn't be terrifying. It should be exciting.

Afterword: Unheard on This Earth

Many believers think that being alone in the cosmos with no god to look after them is terrifying. It's as if this concept causes flashbacks to that time, as toddlers, when they were accidentally separated from their parents in a crowded amusement park, or that night when they suddenly realized that Mommy and Daddy would die someday.

And, while it's perfectly natural to feel childlike fear at the thought of no parents or, in this case, no Sky Daddy watching over us, shouldn't we (as a species) be grown up enough to stand on our own two feet? What's so bad about only having one shot at life without fear or hope for an afterlife? Why can't we be good for goodness' sake?

Yes, that means we'll never get to see our loved ones again in Heaven. And yeah, that means assholes like Adolf Hitler and Osama Bin Laden aren't being roasted in the brimstone barbeque pits of Hell for eternity, as much as they deserve it. But, so what if there's no one up there keeping score? Who cares if nobody's noticing all the good deeds I've been doing? And we should all relax about all the times we've masturbated or how many hangovers we've put ourselves through. Let's just live and learn without fear of a celestial scorekeeper!

To paraphrase the great science fiction author, Harlan Ellison: The universe doesn't *know* you're here. It doesn't *care* about you. The universe just IS.

On the surface that's quite a cold, depressing thought, isn't it? But that's only because most of us have been raised in a culture with characters like Santa Claus, Yahweh, Jesus, and Mohammed. I've heard interviews with folks who were raised in atheist homes who consider the thought of an omnipotent deity claustrophobic, laughable, and ludicrous. To them, everything that I've written about in this memoir will be alien. And, frankly, I find that to be quite cool.

As for me, after being raised Catholic and spending years as a rabid, born again believer, I can either choose to let this reality frighten me back into the secure cage of religion or I can put on my big boy undies and deal with it. At times that's easier said than done. My brain was conditioned, for a good twenty-six years, to believe in a god who's always there for me and an afterlife to look forward to. All of that brainwashing can't be undone overnight. There are fleeting moments when the urge to pray for someone (or request prayers) during stressful times comes over me. But that impulse quickly flickers out because I know that prayer is nothing more than a self-soothing technique that would waste time that could be spent more productively.

Still, on the bright side, knowing that no one's policing my every thought or deed is quite liberating. I can make mistakes, shake my head ruefully at my ineptitude, laugh and move on. Yeah, I lost my temper and kicked an inanimate object in public. Whoop-dee-do! Next time I'll do a better job of controlling my emotions. Hours of my life won't be wasted by beating myself up and repenting endlessly for being human.

And this liberation has led me to be more selfless than ever. Little gestures of kindness make me feel all warm and fuzzy inside, like holding doors open for people or letting them cut in line at the grocery store. The money I used to tithe to churches gets donated to worthy charities. Plus, I thoroughly enjoy volunteering at a center that helps people with mental illnesses. As a Christian I rarely (if ever) did any of these things. It's just easier to get outside my own head now that it's not crowded with the presence of a holy trinity.

As for the afterlife, my wife, who has to deal with the dual agonies of Fibromyalgia and hemiplegic migraines, is fond of saying, "There just HAS to be something better than this. Please tell me this isn't all there is!" If I had to feel like I had the flu everyday and watch every damn thing I ate to avoid headaches (with stroke-like symptoms) then I'd probably feel the same way. Even though I don't believe there's anything other than our short time on this earth I try not to roll my eyes or preach a sermon to my beautiful bride. I did way too much of that when I was born again. It's amazing Missy didn't divorce me!

Of course I'd be a liar if I claimed to have no fear of death. The concept of ceasing to exist scares the shit out of me. Hell, even hearing that a friend's pet died reduces me to tears. But that's just me. I want to live a long life, and I'm a ridiculously sentimental animal lover. Still, knowing that life is short doesn't strip my existence of meaning. It forces me to be more conscious of taking things for granted. There's no guarantee that I'll live another second. I could be a widower tomorrow. My friends and loved ones could die at any time. So the precious, fleeting nature of life creates a sense of urgency about spending my precious time with those who are supportive, loving, open-minded, and appreciative.

Besides, life's WAY too short to waste on assholes.

Let's just live and learn.

66485662R00185

Made in the USA
Lexington, KY
15 August 2017